When Memory Speaks

When Memory Speaks

Timothy Brownlow

Rock's Mills Press
Rock's Mills, Ontario • Oakville, Ontario
2025

Published by
Rock's Mills Press
www.rocksmillspress.com

Copyright © 2025 by Timothy Brownlow.
All rights reserved. No part of this publication may be reproduced, distributed, or transmitted in any form or by any means, including photocopying, recording, or other electronic or mechanical methods, without the prior written permission of the publisher, except in the case of brief quotations embodied in critical reviews and certain other non-commercial uses permitted by copyright law. For permission requests, contact the publisher at:
customer.service@rocksmillspress.com

For adoption, trade, and bulk orders, contact the publisher at:
customer.service@rocksmillspress.com

Rock's Mills Press (both the name and the styling in Rockwell Bold) is a registered trademark and is used under license.

Library and Archives Canada Cataloguing in Publication data has been applied for.

In memory of my courageous parents:
CHARLES EDWARD REGINALD BROWNLOW (1902–1956),
ALICE ELEANOR DUGGAN (1901–1978),
who met adversity with grace and fortitude;
and
ANNE CARRICK, known as NAN (1909–1989),
who was the greatest blessing of my mother's life.

*Extract from the Conclusion of a Poem,
Composed in Anticipation of Leaving School*

Dear native regions, I foretell,
From what I feel at this farewell,
That, wheresoe'er my steps may tend,
And whensoe'er my course shall end,
If in that hour a single tie
Survive of local sympathy,
My soul will cast the backward view,
The longing look alone on you.

Thus, while the Sun sinks down to rest
Far in the regions of the west,
Though to the vale no parting beam
Be given, not one memorial gleam,
A lingering light he fondly throws
On the dear hills where first he rose.

WILLIAM WORDSWORTH

Contents

I
The Baily, Howth, County Dublin ... 1

II
Ballanagh House, Avoca, County Wicklow ... 23

III
65 Wellington Road, Ballsbridge, Dublin 4 ... 53

IV
No Fixed Abode ... 77

V
302 Stong College, York University, Toronto, Ontario ... 91

VI
The Cottage, Caulcott Lodge, Caulcott, Oxfordshire ... 99

VII
Fairbridge Drive, Duncan, British Columbia ... 107

Acknowledgements & A Note about the Author ... 117

I

The Baily, Howth, County Dublin

When memory speaks, what are its early
whisperings? I was six years old, nineteen
forty-seven, just before Christmas,
seated on a sofa before a big
bay window overlooking Dublin Bay.
Frisky waves made smudgy grey brushstrokes
as I scanned the view to follow shipping:
dredgers, pleasure boats (few in this season),
the ferry steamer bound for Liverpool
passing through the main canvas of my sight,
then disappearing into the foreground.
I could run down the road leading to the cliff
and wave at passengers idling on the deck
as the vessel throbbed in close to the point
on which the Baily lighthouse stood its guard,
booming out its foghorn in thick weather.
Across the bay, the mail boat moved slowly
out of Dun Laoghaire harbour, then made
a straight beeline for Holyhead, a place
then as foreign and mysterious
as a location in a fairy story.

Indeed, Britain seemed more distant than
many a fictional place, as I came
to consciousness of my place in the world,
a process never completed, so mixed
was my inheritance. It was in that
window, I stared for hours at a wedding
dress, the one worn by Elizabeth
for her marriage to the handsome Philip;
the work-rich weave of the fabric was stored
up in my inner mind like a token
of complexity in the slow-blooming
awareness of a strange and puzzling world.

So began a continuing quest
for my foothold on the earth, constantly

thrown awry by competing loyalties
and contradictory impressions;
it didn't help that I was a Gemini:
a double-charactered identity
that gave one a shadowy sibling,
one's inner twin commenting on the way
the other half was behaving, careful
watchdog of one's thoughts and aspirations.
There was also an early awareness
of the problematics of existence,
my father having contracted T.B.
soon after I was born, so I never
knew him well, or saw his charismatic
prime, his courageous business enterprise
that gave us for a while an affluence
that took the sting out of his condition,
and got us all brought up successfully.

My mother's life was very difficult,
although the marriage was a blessèd one:
they lost their first child at only four months,
in the year that the Depression began,
after which my father borrowed fifty
pounds from a friend, went to London, and bought
some franchises which were to be a boon
that saw us through our youth. My mother's
third child was a Down's syndrome baby,
who always lived at home, thanks to the deep
love of our second mother, Nan, who was
hired by my mother in nineteen thirty.
Nan became our own Mother Theresa,
a stable North Star of integrity.

It was in that window I listened spell-
bound to the growing and fading sounds of
the early flights to London, as they passed
over the house, slow DC-3s that seemed

to labour through the air, and took six minutes
or so to disappear from sight and sound
on their way to that exotic city.
In May, the adjacent cherry tree
was profusely thickened with pink blossoms,
through which I peered at distant manoeuvrings
of boats in the bay, or massive cloud shapes
building up my fantasy times-to-come.

From that same window, I used a telescope
to spy out part of that time-to-come,
steadying the lens, bringing into focus
my forthcoming school across the bay,
pretentiously adorned with turreting,
a mock-Gothic pile where I was to be
shut up in both senses, my early style
of letters to my sisters, so much admired,
was steam-rollered out of me by correctness
and middle-class convention, an early
case of the troublous task of writing:
at age six or twenty-six, revealing
too much of my inner self to the world,
whether schoolmasters, bankers, clergymen,
or political opponents, radical
deniers of joyous implicit love
or too much musing on the beautiful.

There were some compensations, the cricket field
soaking up my home-sickness, providing
a life-long love of bat and ball, a sense
of speed amidst a lazy-seeming game,
the endless nuance of never-the-same
flightings of the ball, swerving, spinning, full
pitch coming at one to make up your mind
before the mind could get itself in gear.
There I made my first heroes: Ray Lindwall
a wonder with his ninety-mile-an-hour

projectiles, and those West Indians,
Walcott, Weekes, and Worrall, endless stylists
of the cut and slice and pounding straight drives
streaking off the bat with musical slaps
and plonks and plinks, music to my eardrums.

A few years later, at the age of ten,
I discovered another window-view,
being made to close-study works of art
as a kind teacher put before us
classic paintings, Renaissance and nineteenth-
century, instilling a lifelong yen
for distances, painted or real, for tricks
of light enhancing bleak reality
with flecks and points of pigmented focus.
So art, sport, real life got intermingled
in a phantasmagoria of zeal,
a healthy release, never escapist,
because tempered in a well-composed whole.

Another sound provided a rhythmic, hardly
conscious backdrop to my existence:
an electric-powered tram passed behind
our garden fence every few hours,
the irregular clattering of wheels
over rails and points deeply memorized
in some inaccessible hideaway
of the brain, perhaps to be rejolted
into consciousness by some upsetting
emotional event, a landslide spill
unearthing buried shards of past breathings
assembled by the archaeology
of feeling later on. *The Irish Times*
came soaring over the ivy-covered
wall, thrown by Mr. Maypother, leaning
out from the open platform of the tram,
never getting lost in weeds or wild grass,
so punctilious was his projection.

Such devil in the details is our former
life: millions of seemingly empty
experiences, yet each one packed full
of potential like an atom, waiting
to be split into eternal fragments
of inexplicably providential
flashes of being. Wasn't it Thomas
Browne who wrote that no one could see his height,
his altitude, from the outside, so deep
and broad and high was his interior
life, standing on "Atlas his shoulders"?
Thus was the gulf between my inner self
and the self with which I fronted the world,
always inclining me to irony,
so mistaken we can be about
another human being, visible
only to the eye that never blinks,
that inner eye of Buddha-like control.

Swaying out from the pier, the half-full launch
breasted the larger swell at harbour's mouth,
pointing its blunted nose at Ireland's Eye,
a mile offshore, its cliffs pullulating
with raucous sea-birds, gannets, guillemots,
perhaps some puffins, perched on deep-dropping
ledges among the trembling sea-pinks,
inviting childish adventures worthy
of the best pages of Enid Blyton;
kids don't pretend to be literary
snobs, a good yarn is all they need to pull
them into make-believe, invaluable
in later life when reality gets
too real for comfort or invention;
life makes up plots that no genius
could muster, the darkest Gothic nightmares
implicit all the time in our natures.
In his healthy days, my father would skipper

his red-sailed boat out to the island
for children's picnics, sand-and pebble-filled.

Eager to find out where those DC-3s
had come from, I bicycled from Howth Head
out to Collinstown Airport, as it was
known as then, snapped the lumbering take-offs
and tricky landings of each plane, every
new sensation a whole world of transport,
figurative and actual. I could
have cycled on forever, so inspired
was I by the physical exertions
of hill, of flat, the blissful free-for-alls
in letting the bike freewheel down a hill,
sensations almost beyond bodily,
not experienced since, no matter how
much one tries to relive former pleasures.

When does pleasure in the moment start to
transmogrify into something lesser,
when life converts us from young epicures
of the fleeting scene into Puritans
of self-righteousness, deeply committed
to a reductionist mentality,
empowered by knowledge, law, convention,
and all the paraphernalia of
being bland know-it-all-befores, intent
on persuading others that our tiny
peep-hole into the panorama of things
is the one and only paradigm?
The true spiritual task, it seems to me,
involves unravelling that grownupness,
off-casting the bling of self-consciousness
to uncover the essential heartache
of being in the heart of beingness.
Isn't that what Saint Francis meant by "Preach
the Gospel, use words only if you have to"?

A team of workmen digging up our road
to lay a new pipe along the margin:
I asked the foreman if I could join in,
intrigued by the dignity of labour.
So he let me as a favour try out
my puny muscles shovelling the earth,
wheelbarrowing, raking, digging, bending,
sharing banter with the congenial
men, out in all weathers in the real world.
In the evening I went down to chat
with the night-watchman in his sentry-box,
a comforting warmth drifting from the coals
in the brazier, above it a can
of tea simmering all day, its perfume
the most delicate aroma I have
ever encountered. My father colluded
with the foreman, so that at the end
of the week I received a package:
immaculate half-crowns as pocket cash.
Emboldened by my new employment role,
I broke the spell somewhat by requesting
time off to go for a swim: down the cliff
path with its hundred-foot drop, along which
I had ridden my bike, innocent
of danger as I was then, ignorant
of the inexorable, exhausting lives
of those kindly men I imitated,
knowing all along I was for a time
protected from the harshness of the world.

It must have been in nineteen forty-six,
as Ireland began to communicate
with the rest of the world after the lull
of neutrality in a major war,
my father brought me up to the garage
at the top of the drive, slowly peeling
off the tarpaulin that covered the car:

a vintage nineteen-twenties Jaguar
with huge long bonnet, goggle-eyed headlamps,
even separate fog lights in yellow,
a curved skirting-board, mahogany
dashboard, a small button for ignition.
Daddy let me start the beast, surprising
us by coughing into life almost at once.
Out onto the roads with hardly any
other traffic, many pedestrians
and many bicycles, letting me steer
as I sat in his lap, encompassing
the large steering-wheel with horn at centre,
the old leather seats comforting his back.
When eight years later, we moved to Wicklow,
I first experienced sixty m.p.h.
as we galumphed along to a new life,
a blessèd retreat for my ill father,
a paradise for an adolescent
boy with time on his hands on holidays
from school, his milometer notching up
thousands of miles of eager pedalling
to who-cares-what destination, all points
being of equal point and resonance,
all contacts into worlds unrealized.

Recently, watching *The Crown*, I admired
many of the historical details,
down to the cars: the artist who painted
Churchill arrives in a Hillman Minx, poor
cousin of the Humber Super Snipe—Daddy
graduated from one to the other,
depending on the ups and downs of trade,
the Humber a most commodious car,
but not a Rolls, that ultimate symbol
of the effortlessly having-made-it,
or a Daimler with its built-in picnic
equipment in the boot, that families

opened at point-to-points, with rugs and dogs,
laconic gentry pretending to be
ordinary lookers-on, smart chin-scarves
for the women, shooting sticks for the men;
or a Bentley, not quite twin of a Rolls
with its majestic polished pediment.

A life of contrasts, that's what gives us zest,
not just the obvious antimonies—
light and dark, short and long, good and evil—
but the endless relishing of difference,
of diversity, secret of all life:
terra firma after a choppy sea,
a comfy armchair after exertion,
silence after noisy conversation,
or people after too much solitude.
Painters call this feeling *chiaroscuro*—
rough faces lit by sideways candlelight
as in the art of Caravaggio—
the light and shade of things, a siesta
after a wholesome lunch, the slatted light
falling across the sofa, or speckled
leaf-shade beneath overarching trees,
overhearing the trees exchange their words
in organic nature-speak, hard to hear.

Then pleasures of human interaction,
when one finds the ball returned from distant
corners of the court, seemingly an ace.
Conversations used to be more like that,
a physical workout of give and take,
capping each anecdote with anecdote,
building to a climax of amusement
as fragile word-houses were erected
and then dismantled, goals aimed-for and missed.
Thus a true colloquy can imitate
an ideal society, more ear
than mouth, more absorption than aggression.

Listening has gone the way of all art,
hustled out of countenance by loud-mouth
logic of possession, lissena-me
egotism and obliviousness,
the careless offspring of hard-thrusting minds.
Nothing new under the sun: Lao-tzu
advises the wise person to be like
water, yielding, colourless, all-potent
when enough weight has spilled into the trough
to sweep away the noisy chatterers,
replacing them with blessèd quietude.

When we had run down the twisty pathway,
overhung with wild brambles, to the sea
from the cliff path that runs along Howth Head,
where Yeats had brought Maud Gonne, comparing her
to a wild seabird on the bouncing waves—
we threw off our clothes, put on our skimpy
togs, and splashed into the communal pool—
we all knew it as "Jameson's pool"—
a horseshoe of concrete walls with diving
bollard poking up on one side. The tide
seemed to be always out, but sometimes
a full tide would cover the outlines
of the pool, even topping the bollard,
on rough days a joyous thrashing about
in creamy, sudsy water, hoping that
a greedy tide would not pull us far out,
as it did once to my model yacht,
tacking jauntily out of its depth, then
blown back to rocks a hundred yards along.
If we felt adventurous, we could scale
the rocks in the other direction, round
the corner of the cliff, to "Guinness's
pool": a private, still, deep well of water,
much loved by my brother, its darkest depths
a reflection of our daring trespass,
a foretaste of his rebellious youth.

So, a boy of six going on six hundred,
I greedily sought out the winding paths
over the prolific heather on Howth
peninsula, a small promontory
beloved in ancient Irish poetry, where wild
garlic used to grow, where a timeless eye
would have seen Viking longboats round the point,
and seen the Norman foundations of Howth
Castle (and environs), and many later
comings and goings of the human tribe.
Nature was a strong and silent partner,
which seemed to whisper of lost harmonies,
other energies and distant scenes,
and seemed to bless me with Wordsworthian
forecasts and forebodings, well before I
had come across a word of literature.
Indeed, words can often blunt the freshness
of perception, creating a conundrum
where they become a finger pointing at
the moon, not the light of the moon itself:
not just to see things, but to see *through* them
is the aim of all spiritual life.

Nan, our maid of all work, had a running
commentary with my mother all day,
everything from, "'Clare to God, ma'am, he's a right
auld eejit," to "Did you not cook the peas?"
as they catered ceaselessly to our needs,
and never thought twice about the labour.
As Nan said, it was a laugh a minute,
amazing to look back on later as
I think of all their setbacks: rationing,
the war, known then as the Emergency,
sick children, my father coughing up blood,
tantrums, inadequate medical care,
school rules to negotiate, trunks to pack,
Christopher's tuck-box brimming with forbidden

treats; my father and my elder sister
at the window a week before I was born
as Germans mistook Dublin for Belfast,
and bombed the docks with great loss of life,
my mother having to give birth to me,
hoping that a repeat performance was
not in the offing.

                    Wandering the lanes
of Howth Head and the Baily with Leo,
the postman, who liked me to string along
as we delivered the post to far-flung
houses, hidden in dusky shrubberies:
first, The Needles, a Georgian gem,
was always a delight to saunter into,
the grass tennis court newly mown, the maid
gratefully answering the door and chatting;
then Ceanchor House with its veranda,
the view across the bay magnificent,
its gardens spilling down, down the cliff slopes;
and Earlscliffe, where Provost Mahaffy lived
at the time he was tutor to Oscar.

My favourite by far was Roxboro,
Italian arcades running around
the whole house; Madeleine, stone-deaf—
but chatting to a garrulous parrot—
blowing a sports whistle for her servants,
who came from all corners of the garden
as if summoned to angelic feasts.
Tennis parties at Roxboro were like
a scene in an old sepia print,
Madeleine and her bachelor brother,
Harold, the kindest of people—they were
the last of a generation for whom
kind and dignified manners were second
nature, so natural it seemed as if

all one's life one would meet exquisite
care and courtesy; many were like them.
There was much wrong with the world, as always,
but indifferent modern manners is
not a fair exchange for whatever good
we have since achieved; so I am glad that
my impartial ten-year-old gaze was taking
everything in. The tram would clatter by, its
wires connected by a swaying pulley-
like contraption, sizzling with endeavour.

Then there was Edros, with a goldfish pond
just inside the gate, a long avenue
with a hedge I never saw more than one
inch too long uncut. Pat, the housekeeper,
was a close confederate of our Nan:
between them nothing in the neighbourhood
escaped their capacious gossip-hungry
attention: "Did you see Pat out o' Massers?"
Nan would call from the pantry as I put
my bike away, eager for people-news,
never forgotten, even when she came
thirty years later to stay with us in
Canada, the tape recorder getting
hot with overuse as she "gosthered"
away, while tweaking our bull-terrier,
Tommy, with a wooden kitchen spoon.

One day, on the way back along the cliff
to home, I took a cut through a private
garden, the majestic lawn of Edros
as it spilled down to the cliff-top, lopping
several hundred yards off the usual
trip, as recounted by my mother
later: "Mrs. Masser was having tea,
and sees a tiny figure marching through
the grass as if he owned it all; 'that must

be Timothy,' says she in amusement."
They were close family friends, but even
so, a child has to learn the niceties
of boundaries, soft and hard, that even
paradise has limits, prohibitions,
that punctiliousness is the keynote
of surviving in this gobsmacking world.

Talking of limits, I remember how
the builders measured out the ground with string
for our new neighbours, the Browns, then trenches
for the foundations—no more corncrakes
were heard in that field, their piercing cries gone
into memory limbo—Hastings Brown
and I would take a dip together
in the sea pools: arrived back at our door,
Nan would greet us with "Hastings, Hastings, get
the bastings," and sticky-out-ears Hastings
would giggle and go pink. They were millers,
and Hastings and I showed off each other's
family businesses, their clacketing mill,
and the buzzing machinery of my dad's
spark-plug factory. We moved from Howth soon after
the Browns arrived, with their Austin
Seven, that snub-nosed pride of fifty-two,
with its jaunty striped A on the bonnet,
and smell of brand-new upholstery, sign
of wealth, as most cars were second-hand,
and soon lost that fresh-leather aroma.
How devastating looking back can be,
as I realize that I never saw
Hastings again, that when one is young one
thinks that time is on one's side, that the years
to come stretch out in regular array
as opposed to Baudelaire's awareness
of smallness "à la clarté des lampes."

What fun I had with Bridgy and Bessie
and Nan as they went about their housework:
throwing balls of plasticine around,
Bessie giving as good as she received
and collapsing in mountainous giggles
in a kitchen chair: "Timody, you'll
kill me with the laughter one o' these days."
When Bessie died, her husband proudly sent
the hearse on a circuitous journey
all around the Hill of Howth, so many
people loved her and waved at the cortège.

Nan, alas, died in nineteen eighty-nine,
one of her last requests being that same
wooden spoon well-polished from Tommy-bashing;
Pat out o' Massers lasted well into
her nineties, cherished by the family.
The Irish do funerals well. When my
sister died, we left the undertaker's
yard on a Joycean street in Dublin,
(the company features in *Ulysses*),
and slowly followed the hearse through north-side
suburbs, men outside pubs sweeping their hats
off or crossing themselves, what matter
that it was a Protestant funeral?
Before setting off, we were treated to jokes
by the undertaker boss, a seasoned
connoisseur of burials; he often
felt like telling the oldest mourners:
"It's hardly worth your while going home."

Age eleven, I was drifting to sleep,
anticipating the soporific
tram cacophony, when Nan came in, picked
up the framed photograph of my slightly
older cousin Kevin, who already
in his teens showed that extraordinary

concentration on a single goal
that was to lead to a Lifetime Oscar.
He was taken by his worried parents
on a trip to Paris, to divert his mind
from "childish" slapstick movies—his homework
falling behind. Far from playing tourist,
Kevin hunted through old movie archives
and found a forgotten reel of Abel
Gance's nineteen-twenties' masterpiece
Napoleon, which he spent sixty years
restoring and slow-piecing together.
Such near-impossible goals were held up,
such lifelong slow-burning obsessionals.

My mother loved old-fashioned rose bushes;
a stroll around the garden brought drifting
scents to the nostrils—or hard-pedalling
my bike around and around the rose beds
until the lawn was worn and tracked, outcries
from Nan to get on outa that and go
to create mischief elsewhere or she'd give
me a clatther about the ears. I would
love sitting in one of my father's deck chairs
(kept in the garden house for him to get
some fresh air), especially in rain storms,
with a tough rug or two over my head,
being out in the elements, with swoosh
of churning trees nearby, labouring boats
in the bay dipping their bows into wave troughs
and slowly rising again, shuddering.

Like many children, I was a devout
collector: cigarette cards, and the silver
lining that used to wrap those killer "fags,"
as they were called; when nearly everyone
smoked in private or in public, many
people got through two packs or more a day.

I hunted down those wallets of matches
called book matches: on visits to London
with my parents, I would rush into each
hotel or posh-looking restaurant,
usually emerging triumphant,
while the salespeople indulgently smiled.
I had hundreds of them, but the tea chest
holding my collection was mistakenly
thrown out during one of our household moves.

My second eldest sister was the beauty
of the family—when we were on
holiday on Lake Geneva, a man
asked the waiter to be placed looking straight
at her—those were the bad old days of male
gazing, a time of surface innocence—
it was late summer, nineteen fifty-one—
my mother not knowing quite what to think
of this older gentleman, maybe he
was just a connoisseur of beauty.
Aunt Gladys took black-and-white photographs
of that holiday, my sister raven-
haired and sharp-profiled, laughing, my brother
at his happiest floating on his back,
family unity never to be
so enjoyed by all those in the snap.

Vevey, Lausanne, Montreux, old-fashioned trams
went jostling slowly between them, tickets
nicked at the edge with a clipper, so that
our journeys were notched up like souvenirs;
the novelty of *croissants* for breakfast,
my greedy boyhood used to big fry-ups
gradually acquired a taste for
continental breakfasts, with their weak tea,
jams and wonderful bread. We took the train
into Italy and spent idyllic

days exploring Lago Maggiore,
my sister screaming at the quick lizards,
admiring the shimmering, hot lake-scapes,
the terraces of white, hidden villas
that had me dreaming again that life
could be like this, given a lot of luck.

We would take mountain walks, colour-coded,
some leading through high meadows, the cow-bells
clacking and tinkling at different heights
and directions; some led deep into woods
with sudden vistas of steep alp on alp
and hidden waterfalls talking somewhere.
When I later read Wordsworth's walking tour
of the Alps in *The Prelude*, I was there
immediately, no matter that deep time
and harsh history separated us.

In the Swiss capital, Bern, the gentle
Aare seen from sturdy bridges, many squares
with central fountains spouting on silent
afternoons, everyone behind shutters.
Then on to Basel, the all-mighty Rhine
forcing its long passage to the North Sea.
I took roll after roll of photographs
with my box-camera, the prints tiny
with serrated edges, the negatives
tokens of life to be still developed.

Then a visit to Château de Chillon,
with its damp dungeons, its Byronic mood
of defiance, stuck out on a rocky
promontory, as the delayed back swell
from the passing pleasure boats exhausted
itself against the rocks. The swell was more
exhilarating as one paddled in
those tourist contraptions floating one out

a hundred yards into the lake, feeling
the wash from nearby steamers dipping by.

One afternoon in two thousand and six
my sister and I took a cruising boat,
after a long lunch of *perche à l'orange*
on the quayside at Vevey, past Chillon
with people waving handkerchiefs from its
turrets. Later we walked along the wall
atop the promenade, and found the beach
where a happy family once sported
in blissful obliviousness of time.
A single swan swam round the ragged wall,
and only Proust could then delineate
the complex mixture of wheels within wheels
that overcame me as I ingested
the lapping waves of time after slow time
that washed against my innermost beachhead.

II

Ballanagh House, Avoca, County Wicklow

In the summer of nineteen fifty-three
I made it to the first eleven
cricket team; we walked in "crocodiles"
to Killiney Beach and ate cream-puff
buns and tepid tea out of heavy flasks
on the day of the Coronation;
our headmaster was a loyal West Brit.,
a word I only learned much later,
no divisions, inner or outer, yet
in my quest for an integrated life.

When my parents collected me in July,
instead of heading north around the bay,
we went south through Bray, Kilmacanogue,
Newtownmountkennedy, Ashford, and turned
right towards Avoca before Arklow.
My first sight of our new house was delight,
mixed with sad awareness that my father
had bought it as a country retreat
to sweeten his final years. Otherwise,
things were opening up: discovery
of Beethoven; a glimpse of the Oval
Test Match against Australia: Denis
Compton going down on one knee to sweep
the ball to glory, the field over-swarmed
at once by eager fans. The best version
was on the Pathé newsreel in the local
cinema, the earliest TV sets
in other people's houses never free
of interference and flickering "snow".

When we first arrived as "runners-in",
my father took me to the village pub,
two miles away in Avoca, later
famous as the *Ballykissangel* pub.
The then owner had a superb array
of match boxes which adorned every inch

of wall space and more; he doled out advice
on where to find the best ones, whetting my
collector's appetite for augmentation.
From age twelve to eighteen, this lucky boy
was inheritor of this fair seed time,
darkened and exalted by my father's death.

One day at Ballanagh my sister and I
returned from walking through Ballyarthur,
avenues winding, dipping through pastures
scattered with sheep, one eminent chestnut
a prototype of Samuel Palmer's
painting (discovered later), a magic
evocation of pastoral, so far
removed from modern sensibilities,
but catching perfectly what I felt then,
a sense of completeness in my feelings
that later life so rarely gives, so stuck
are we in fulfilling expectations,
both our own and others', yet never quite
hitting the mark, the feel of true virtue
in its original sense, a bull's-eye
of satisfaction, a torn scattering
of bullet-holes near the target centre.
Anyway, when we came back from our walk,
we looked in the morning room bay window,
anticipating the coal fire blazing
in the grate, and saw an enormous pig
sunning itself before the fire, trotters stretched
out straight like a dog, blissed out by the warmth.

And talking of bulls, one day my sister
was walking in the neighbouring estate,
Shelton Abbey, and we all got worried
that she seemed to be very late coming
back, so my brother and I took the Hillman Minx
out along the interminable lane-

ways of the Earl of Wicklow's demesne—
in Ireland, a domain is a demesne;
I used to explore Howth Castle demesne,
blossom-profuse in ever-fresh May—
and after much blaring of the speeding
horn and arriving at many culs-de-sac,
we find my sister and a friend crouching
behind a tree, while being stared and snorted
at by a huge bull. We bring the Hillman
as far as we can into the wide field,
and Liz and Sue make a quick run for it,
jumping into the swaying car in time.

I see a teenage boy gallivanting
through fields and lanes of rural Wicklow,
the gentle curve of a half-ploughed hillside
entered into his inviolable
open mind-sky, its imprint foretelling
dreamed-of configurations of content.
What matter if many fantasy scenes
never came into actuality,
it is enough that they were once a promise
of a fuller, more immaculate life,
and therefore played a part in one's story?
These joys were always backgrounded by stern
reminders of fragility, weakness,
intimations of mortality
like the passing of dark clouds over the sun,
sending shivers flickering from shoulder
to small of back, so great the contrast
between the light and dark of things, Herbert's
"sour-sweet days" lived intensely from the start.

Home from boarding school for the holidays,
I would run down the vegetable garden
to the greenhouse, numerous household cats
sunning themselves in the bright odorous

atmosphere, the black and white of their fur
scented with grape-and tomato-rich earth,
their cold noses wet as they butted me
with habitual affection. Four weeks
of freedom, cats, bike rides, dogs and donkeys,
what more could a growing boy want?

Multiple voices reach me from the past,
sometimes in a confused shrill chattering,
like jungle parrots frightened by a noise,
other times a silent confidential
colloquy, whether it's all in my mind
or a real conversation of spirits
is in truth immaterial; the past
is always present to those who live well
in the moment, as each moment unfurls
the curling fronds of antique mystery.
And let this take place in silence, silence
cures our everlasting deafness, silence
allows the music of the spheres to sound,
spite of "this muddy vesture of decay."

Among the treasured relics shored up
from the depredations of passing time
I have a framed watercolour, painted
one day in April nineteen fifty-nine:
I had been painting landscapes for years,
but really got it right that day, soft curves
of the Wicklow mountains in their distant
haze, while my brother and sister played ball
with two dogs on the semi-foreground lawn,
framed by the line of stone barns and cottage.
I was sitting in the small garden shed
which doubled as a makeshift gazebo—
what a lovely English word, also in
Hiberno-English: "She made a holy
show in that gazebo of an outfit"—

from which my dreams could spring board,
my faith in life intact, my gratitude
well-exercised in its pace and power.
Never had I seen my mother happier,
in spite of my father's death three years before,
and never had she had such loyal friends.
"Embrace me then, ye hills, and close me in"—
such a Wordsworthian boyhood was mine.

My sister and I used to paint outdoors,
she gifted with a natural graphic
ability, catching cats in many
poses, back leg in the air as they washed,
and all the charming configurations
of animals at rest and at play. What pure
unrepeatable hours and afternoons
thus passed in innocent concentration,
the illusion of youth that they would be
the first of many, yet life is frugal
in its prodigality, happiness
doled out in little parcels, like gruel
grudgingly spooned out to workhouse paupers
in the Dickensian nature of the world.
Thus early on the lesson was made clear,
moments good or bad never come again,
nature has a diabolical way
of inventing a disinherited
awareness, so seize, seize the day, but not
so hard that the moment is stabilized
too soon, and thus loses its nonchalance.

This balancing act is surely what art,
music, literature is concerned with, not
so much the glum lessons of politics,
collective sermons in how to survive,
certainly salutary, but not the core
of most memorable works; above all,

the greatest works of art delineate
a fundamental tenderness: Rembrandt
in his final portraits, self and other,
where the paint is part and parcel of life,
silent pigments broadcasting their ever-
expanding solidarity of love.
Late Shakespeare, where the verse becomes opaque,
and yet more transparent (don't ask me how),
the rhythms ever more imprintable
on our psyches, those motions of the wind
that Wordsworth felt blowing through the words
in great poetry. Late Bach and Beethoven,
"beyond the beyond," as the Irish say,
that aria in the Saint Matthew
Passion where Joseph of Arimathea
comes to bury Jesus, imploring God
to "Mache dich, mein Herze, rein." Such things
sustain an incalculable value.

At Christmas time in nineteen fifty-six
we asked a Hungarian family
to spend two weeks in an Irish home—
Russia had just invaded Hungary.
My mother was superb, dispensing gifts
from our Christmas tree, the log and coal fires
kept cheerfully going, necessitating
many trips to the dark and spooky sheds,
piles of good coal and piles of slack to damp
down an overactive blaze, so comforting
as dusk descended and the garden trees
faded into invisibility,
and the flickering fire cast its jagged
reflections around the walls, ideal
for conversation or for day-dreaming,
dogs snoring before the heat, the Dutch tiles
of the fireplace a faint blue and white, brass
fenders and tongs glowing clean in the dusk,

Beethoven or jazz on the gramophone.

The local priest in Arklow took care
of their pastoral needs—he had grown up
in Austria, had fought in the Luftwaffe,
was witty, cultivated, and well read—
he and I became close friends for decades—
and accompanied our disparate group
for Christmas carols and Anglican hymns,
his profile handsome in an old snap-shot.

I was made nervous by such perfection,
circumstances such as these so rare.
So privileged to be cosy and safe,
as I felt on listening to the weather
forecast on BBC, with its Dogger
and Rockall, Hebrides, images of
raging northern seas, the frail hulls driven
into havens like Ancient Mariner
narratives, exposure and protection
in extremis— how blessed was one's own calm
existence, free from weather, invaders,
and all the thousand natural shocks in
abeyance for the time being. Sufficient
unto the day thereof, why not enjoy
perfection as it comes and goes, ebbs and flows
like those embracing waters fidgeting
around the dim edges of one's consciousness,
biding their time, as inevitable
as that comforting dusky light outside
that pervades the unlit room with softness.

Every mealtime was an event for me;
I always paused in anticipation,
extending a supplicating hand
to the ether like the scene in *The Great
Gatsby* when Gatsby sighs his body

towards the other shore. Like Keats, I felt
that good things could never last, that fate must
be propitiated, be mollified,
keen to show my humble gratitude
to whatever God or power was in charge.
I early made up my mind that life was
dark, that any relief from suffering
was the best one was likely to get,
so even little things gave me deep joy
since they were sure tokens of victory
in this battle-ground of one's inner self.
The song of hidden blackbirds at evening
seemed to agree, so melancholy,
so poignant were their cries, ushering in
the prolific dark, when all would be still,
the air rain-scented, mist-tinged, lung-filling,
a scene indescribably delicious.

Pictures: I was more intuitive
with art and music in my long childhood
than with literature. Art took me first
into other realms of beauty and cliff-
hanging perspectives—think medieval
cosmic visions of the saved and the damned,
the howling, gaping mouths, dainty devils
wielding pitchforks, and so on; heavenly
vistas crowded with overfed *putti*
and earnest-looking disciples gazing
up at serene, self-possessed virginal
beauties, sure at having scaled spiral steps
towards a more-than-blissful lasting goal:
Glückseligkeit: can that word be Englished?

Music next: hard to tell what tonal phrase
set my pulses going, but it must have
been an off-beat melody, the kind that
emanates so effortlessly from Bach,

who specializes in that missing-step
feeling, setting up sweet expectations,
then to stagger them with syncopation,
a momentary trip-me-upness.
As for ecstasy, David Oistrakh playing
Mozart's Fifth Violin Concerto
sounded the heights and depths of emotion
at just the right time, the yellow Deutsche
Grammophon Gesellshaft sleeve with folding flap
is imprinted on my young retina,
along with all the surrounding landscape—
The Ballanagh wheat fields backed by beech trees—
of the day I first heard it in mono
sound but stereoscopic perception.

Music was a most constant companion,
my growing awareness coinciding
auspiciously with long-playing records,
mono and stereo. For my fourteenth
birthday I woke up to sense a presence
in the dawn light, and saw a gleaming bust
of Beethoven atop the new gramophone—
my first real hero for his defiance,
integrity, and astonishing gifts,
his achingly beautiful melodies,
the Violin Concerto heard that year
with Yehudi Menuhin, whose string broke,
so he had to start again: such aplomb.

I remember one superb recital
at school, when Joseph Groocock, our gifted
organist, invited one of the great
performers of that time, Susi Jeans,
to play for a small group of teenagers.
She played Bach's "Wedge" prelude and fugue, treading
out the widening theme with sensible
shoes, her authority unmistakable,

catching Bach's extraordinary blend
of transcendence and down-to-earthness:
Bacchus lurking within Apollo's grove.
What is meant by the morality of art?
A stillness born of a perfect balance
between extremes of self-expression,
self-transcendence into something higher,
a lasting, vivid orientation
of the self towards the ineffable,
trembling on the brink of comprehension,
but always groping onwards in the dark,
the dark of brightness itself, a searchlight
of the mind condensed into true focus.

From singing in the chapel choir at school
I got to know Bach chorales in every part:
treble, alto, tenor, and bass as my voice
deepened, and held these harmonies ever
in my mind, anchors for my fickle nerves
as I negotiated growing up
in all its disillusionments, mistakes,
confident that harmony underlay
all vicissitudes, all dystopias;
by our own courage are we justified.
Do you recognize the rhythm in that
line, thanks to Wordsworth, Seamus Heaney?
"By our own spirits are we deified."
"In oils and brushwork are we ratified."
Artists borrow what they can get away with;
it won't work if it is too far-fetched
or straining credulity, but if it
is thoroughly assimilated,
it energizes, like wholesome foodstuffs,
the generic heritage of language.

Words, words, words. The tidal word energy
of Dickens—fuelled by manic walking,

often at night—swept me away with it.
One Christmas holiday I brought *Bleak House*
home to read in vivid short episodes
between walks, music, and decorating
the tree, or driving my mother to Arklow,
where she would meet friends for tea, and rummage
among the seed shelves in Annesley's,
planning her garden layout. One always
paid in cash in those days, the coins and bills
tucked into a little bowl, sent buzzing
on wires to the central cash receiver,
who clinked in the right change, sent it whizzing back.
Ireland was decently old-fashioned, more
Edwardian than modern, everything
personalized, with dignified manners
at all levels, not just the well-to-do.
Mr. Annesley was always at hand,
with helpful advice, enquiries after
family members; my sister Rose loved
that shop, and would chat away for ages
while I lingered in the background, letting
my deep brain imprint itself unbeknownst.

Or I would wait in the car, quick-snatching
a few more pages of Dickens, a shot
of that verbal energy, those rhythms
a controlled torrent of words, characters
caricatures of themselves: Uriah Heep,
"I'm an 'umble man, Master Copperfield,"
and Mr. Micawber, ever hopeful
and ever feckless, and his stalwart wife,
"I never will desert Mr. Micawber."
My favourite was Peggotty, shining
a light for Master Copperfield, as Nan
did for me: "My darlin' boy, my darlin' boy,"
she exclaimed towards the end, thousands
of miles away. She is sealed upon my heart,
"upon mine arm, for love is strong as death."

Music, family, books, conversation,
the older generation to gawk at—
I was the baby of the family—
their cars, their clothes, their grown-up lifestyles,
gave me much to ponder. It was the age
of Dior, Hubert de Givenchy, Audrey
Hepburn, Grace Kelly and her princely beau,
when famous people usually had style,
and didn't have to claim celebrity
or even fabulous wealth to get by,
when intellectuals had some presence
and universities were venerated.
After seeing *Rear Window*, I was dumb
with hopeless adolescent hankering
for such pert diction: Kelly's line after
she goes to an inner room to change: "Preview
of coming attractions," provoking deep
turmoil to my hormones more than any
explicit come-hither sensuousness.

As for Hepburn, the epitome
of chic, no wonder Colette fell in love
at first sight: "Who is that enchanting girl?"—
Audrey was practising dance-steps, believing
herself unseen, but Colette happened to
pass by the door, peripherally
sensing that she should look again—ka-boom!
There she had discovered the perfect Gigi.

One afternoon in nineteen fifty-six
my sister and I were asked to luncheon
with the Wynne sisters, all in their eighties,
who managed between them a thriving mill
producing woollen clothes and woven goods,
with colours tinctured with local plant life—
their yellow seemed straight off the mountain gorse.
On our way out through the antique hallway,

my sister saw a crudely tied parcel
with BALENCIAGA, Paris, scrawled in
spidery, inky writing. Quality
can be found in unexpected places:
the dyer's art subdued to its element.

What pleasure my mother got from house-guests:
she'd be scraping and kneading and banging
in the kitchen for days before, so that
on the day the house looked spruced-up, flower-
bedecked, polished and vacuumed—Nan would cry,
"Get out o' me way while I'm hooverin."
My elder sister's wedding in fifty-
seven was a joyous extension of
the usual conscientiousness,
every detail thought through, every moment
accounted for: when Nan caught some young male
obstreperous guests purloining champagne
bottles from the pantry cupboard, she snapped:
"You wouldn't rob a widow-woman, would you?"
They retreated, suitably abashed.

A feeling of pre-modernity gave
one's interactions a ritualized
assurance: "A grand evening indeed,"
as one passed old men on the footpath;
or "What can I do you for?" entering
a tailor's to order a new shirt.
Gossip started: "Come here 'til I tell you";
a twenty-time-told joke: "Did ye'ever hear
the wan about…?" "Yeah, yeah, yeah," one kept to one-
self and swallowed too much beer for fear
of offence, or choked oneself trying not
to laugh at the wrong bits. "How's your mother?"
would invariably be asked at every
shop she frequented, her gait and shape
often compared to the Queen Mother,

a little low-slung, but impeccably
dressed, her idiosyncratic choices
of foodstuffs meticulously recalled:
"Timmy likes marmalade for his sausages;
it must be Little Chip from Findlater's."
At the local cinema, the man who
took the tickets as one entered the fog
of Woodbine smoke drifting over the screen,
greeted my mother, "Here comes the wise old owl."

Nineteenth of May, nineteen fifty-six:
confirmation day, Anglican service
at school, the Archbishop presiding,
confirmandi in their clean surplices,
polished shoes and immaculate collars,
all lined up awaiting the laying-on
of hands, bread and wine of first communion.
Nan was there (in spite of anathema
of Catholic dogma that we were errant
heretics); she wasn't going to miss it.
Thank God for people full of character
who surrounded me in my long childhood;
no matter what I learned or didn't learn at school,
they were as comforting as the ancient
hills and rocks and heathers of my ramblings.

After lunch in Bentley's of Molesworth Street,
my brother and brother-in-law took me
to a stadium on the South Circular
Road; I was puzzled by their excitement.
Two hours later, my mind was forever changed
by the laser blast of Armstrong's trumpet,
by Trummy Young's trombone, and all the skill
of the All Stars, legendary players.
We then drove out to County Meath, to Trim,
to Auntie Nellie's farm for afternoon
tea, my brain pulsing with what I had heard.

Then it was back to school, evening chapel,
my choirboy surplice donned again, the hymns
ringing out with extra zest, my treble
voice required to do the extra descants.
God, family, music, food, discipline:
such things set the pace for adolescence.

My first term at secondary boarding
school, in spite of being told to beware
of over-interested senior boys,
I accepted a challenge to ransack
apple trees in the neighbouring estate
of Marlay Grange. My partner-in-crime
and I scaled the crumbling old wall, creeping
through long grass, and found the hanging ripe fruit
easily, stuffing our pockets full. Then,
a race back to the perimeter wall,
and safely back to the confines of school.
This raid into the Garden of Eden
was, as far as I know, never revealed,
but I notched it up to experience,
secretly glad to be initiated
into some of the rituals of youth.

When we had paraded out of chapel,
we lined up in the cloisters to allow
masters and prefects to run the gauntlet
of our eyes and ears, the Senior Prefect's
slightly uneven gait in formal shoes
forever etched in my long memory;
he used to practise his cricket batting
strokes on the lawn of Chapel Quadrangle
just below my new-boy bed, as I dreamed
of home, or of eventually
lording it as a prefect, a mattress
hanging out the window of his special
room on a glorious summer afternoon.

Life is full of hierarchies, good and bad,
to be enjoyed or challenged according
to the circumstances, never stable.

He came soon afterwards to play cricket
at Ballyarthur, in a brief period
when a group of my brother's friends rallied
some few-and-far-between enthusiasts,
two teams to negotiate the bumps
and slopes of an improvised cricket pitch.
My father paid for and had constructed
a makeshift corrugated pavilion,
where lunch and tea would be served, shelter
for the "rain stopped play" intervals, feature
of all outdoor activities, a fickle
climate spoiling picnics, tennis matches,
the lawn tennis courts all-vulnerable.

Aunt Gladys, known to the kids as Cha-cha,
would drive down at weekends, take photographs,
and listen patiently to all our woes
and wisecracks, blowing her cigarette smoke
strongly towards the ceiling, as if to
imply, I know I shouldn't be smoking;
but everyone smoked then, it was a sign
of sophistication, gestures nourished
by every "film" or "picture", as we
called the movies—that Humphrey Bogart cool,
that James Stewart drawl, Mickey Rooney dash.
When did hats suddenly go out of style?
In old photographs, all the men have hats,
subtle class distinctions built in to each,
even down to the amount of tilt allowed.

Joy in the physicality of sport:
nothing ever replaced those visceral
experiences of golf course, cricket

and rugby pitch, hockey lawn, tennis court,
or managing a stitch as one plodded
over hillside, bog and gorse-strewn terrain
on a five-mile crosscountry, hard thudding
back down the Hurley Lane above the school
and collapsing to vague hand claps beside
the chapel. Such youthful exaltations:
everything then seems a preparation,
a foretaste for what really never comes,
or not, at any rate, in the disguise
one had imagined or forecasted it.
All the more valuable to keep
sensations fresh, even into old age—
falling slowly sideways as the cricket
ball curves its parabola from a fast
delivery catching the outside edge
of the bat, still in the air as my hand
outstretched intercepts its perfect falling,
a consummation of desire and flight.
The ball firmly lodged in my stinging palm,
I stumble to my feet, oblivious
of cries of "Good catch, boy," deep absorbing
the never-again-so-luminous clouds.

I remember seeing in some cricket book
a scorer's diagram of Len Hutton's
legendary knock, in nineteen thirty-nine,
of three hundred and sixty-four, not out,
how Hutton exploited every corner,
slicing, driving, slashing, easing, coaxing
the ball into every crevice between
alert fielders, throwing themselves sideways
to intercept impossibly precise
trajectories. On paper, it looked like
a sketch of some architectural plan
from Vasari's or Leonardo's hand,
a mandala, a poetic of space,

a lesson in conserving energy
by utilizing every sleight of wrist
and peripheral trick of wide-angled
sight, a dance of fancy footwork and quick
reactions, movements so high resolution,
they merge with the pure instinctual:
"Such harmony is in immortal souls."

Racketing down in makeshift toboggans
crunched to a halt by bramble bush or rock,
more bruises notched up on one's soft belly—
schoolboy frolics in the snow, a Breughel
scene as noticed by a passing black crow,
all smudgy white with stumbling figurines
going about their tiny amusements.
Back in dormitory that night, got caught
out of bed at the wrong time, sour prefect
trying to justify his sad duty:
"This hurts me more than it hurts you." Like hell,
one thought as one bent over to receive
two or three sharp stinging lashes. Bruises
now on belly and on backside, as I
proudly displayed to my mother the day
I went home for my father's funeral.
Corporal punishment was much preferred
to sitting in on sunny afternoons
copying out a Tennyson poem,
or irregular Latin constructions.

How I loved those makeshift cricket matches,
a battered rubbish bin for stumps, tennis
ball instead of those sewn cork and leather
sweet-smelling projectiles in the real game.
Then there was cloister cricket, steps leading
up to chapel across the quadrangle
served as wicket, with crudely drawn chalk marks,
the various apertures provided

by each curving section of the cloister
gave one's strokes an extra challenge: how to
catch a ball early so that it could soar
for six over the high schoolroom rooftop,
sometimes never to be seen again.
Or, best of all, a wholesome, floating shot
sent into the recesses of the Warden's
garden, with its rose bushes and brick paths.
Once again, I always knew that such things
never come again, that being grown-up
means becoming self-conscious of such joys,
and therefore one can murder them at birth.
One might ask, is it worthwhile growing up,
and answer that it's not if one cannot
keep "un petit morceau de ciel" above
one's head at all times, bright or overcast.

Quotations fell about my consciousness
like soft rain; always interested in
languages, I relished German, Irish,
French, Latin, or Middle English dictions,
an early escaper from the science
laboratory, with its acrid smells.
I must have been to many an arty
freak, but I gravitated easily
to music, literature, and painting
as my proper element, not thinking
of financial consequences, later
to loom so large, but I chose what I loved
and stuck with it, *amor fati* indeed.
Blame the scholars who recited to me
their internalized enthusiasms:
the themes of poetic melancholy—
"*où sont les neiges d'antan*"—deeply soothing;
then the German of Annette von Droste-
Hūlshoff, or the Latin of Cicero,
and most of all, the spring-time melody

of Geoffrey Chaucer, falling on his knees
to worship a daisy in Anglo-French.
My trouble was I loved too profoundly
to be able to choose a single course,
so it took many setbacks to unhinge
me from my obsessional day-dreamings,
deciding on the plane to Canada
that I must whittle down my character
to a sharp ambitious point, a needle
arrow quivering on my self-compass
until it settled into something firm,
calm, collected, enough of this drifting
round in foolish amateur penumbras.

Christopher at breakfast: "Are you coming
over to Munny with me?" After lunch
we set off in the Hillman Minx, over
the cattle grid with a slow shuddering,
past Ballyarthur House, then the twisting
hairpinned descent to the Woodenbridge golf
course, checking if anyone was playing
in our direction, over the wooden
bridge, beginning to sag, then took the road
along the river to Tinahely,
Carnew, Tullow, turned in the avenue
of Munny House, a pale yellow farmhouse
from which issued the voice of Eartha Kitt;
hoots of laughter as Christabel greeted Dan—
Christopher's school nickname from the comic
character "Desperate Dan" in the *Beano*—
and me, as formidable as she was
when she confronted the Nazis to save
her husband, suspected of being part
of the July plot against Hitler.
Fortunately, they escaped those cruel
clutches, and came to Ireland to begin
afresh with a beautiful working farm.

Dan was at school with the elder two sons,
I with the younger one. Those carefree trips
were a welcome break from worries at home,
as my father had intermittent bouts
of cliff-hanging sickness, the doctor's car
a regular sight as it trundled down
our winding drive—Dan was at his best then,
before my father's death catapulted
him into the family business.
It was Christabel who also played us
Bruno Walter's rehearsals of Mozart's
Symphony Number 36, the "Linz,"
with its wonderfully melodious
slow movement, etched into my memory
by repeated playings with the small score,
such a joy to follow the viola,
counterpointed so mozartfully
in sighs of melancholy happiness;
that cultivated accent of *mittel
Europa,* as Walter ticked off the second
violinists: "Open string, do I hear?
That is a terrible sin in Mozart.
I begin once more, my friends … shimmering."

It will be interesting to see how
a prodigy such as Alma Deutscher,
her purity of childhood unsullied,
will develop into adulthood,
whether the present norms of necessary glumness
will shackle and extinguish her spirit,
already praised as a female Mozart,
or whether her admirable *savoir
faire* will inoculate her against all
jealousy, too much self-awareness,
leaving her free to create a female
stronghold in a very male dominion—
"I don't want to be Mozart, just Alma."
Praise be to that end, and happy journey.

Arklow, a pleasant town with a well-known
boatbuilding yard, a harbour into which
the Vikings must have sailed, navigating
the tide famous for its salt-fresh-water mix,
sea-water meeting the Avoca River.
I lost many a golf-ball in its upstream depths,
and indeed found even more as they lurked
glimmering like fossils between the stones.
The ninth hole ran along the riverbank,
the tenth hole the local bar at Woodenbridge,
where silent men played billiards, and Guinness
was the silent reward for exhaustion.
The room smelt heavily of tobacco,
the leather benches squeaking, torn and patched,
wet fur of tired dogs sleeping at one's feet;
when somebody said something, the dogs stirred
in their sleep, obviously hyper-tuned
to the intonations of human speech,
and went back to doggy science fiction.

Our region of County Wicklow was full
of eccentrics: one friend of my mother's,
from a grand English background, so frugal
with her cooking that her husband once asked
my sister, there for a week to caretake,
to cook him an omelette to make up
the deficit. The two of them sat down
to a creation of twenty-two eggs.
Some people, if one called in before noon,
were already half way through the daily
bottle of whiskey. The walk through the woods
to Avoca was one we didn't make
in dusk or dark: about halfway down,
high-snarling Irish wolfhounds pressed against
the protective wire between oneself
and a dozen mouthfuls of sharp teeth;
a gnome-like man was employed to cut up

donkeys for their food, so we hurried on,
glad to hear the barking din peter out.

The old-fashioned Irish telephone book
was very slim in nineteen fifty-five,
front part for Dublin, then the provinces.
We were Avoca 29, and friends were
Coolkenna 4. All calls went through the post-
mistress's domain, so very little
was secret; my father was on the phone
to a business associate, and said
to him: "I think someone's listening in,"
when an aggrieved voice piped up, "I *am* not."
Another time my mother rang a friend,
but was calmly told by the post-mistress,
"She's not in, I've just seen her walking by."
When Ireland broke away from British rule
in nineteen twenty-two, the post-boxes
were painted green, the embossed cyphers
with Queen Victoria's insignia
were left intact, and to this day no-one
has bothered to change the names of the Royal
Irish Automobile Club, the Royal
Irish Yacht Club, and the best hotel then
in central Dublin was known as the Royal
Hibernian. My parents never talked
about the nineteen twenties, and we were
blissfully ignorant of those rough times,
Southern Protestants wondering what place
would be left for them in the general
reshuffling. I was in my seventies
when I learned that my mother's uncle
had been accosted in his chemist's shop
by two IRA men, and when he failed
to deliver, they shot him dead right there.
We were taught to love the Ireland that we
knew, a sweet place for a happy childhood,

with no sense of us and them, no rancour,
before the fall into division,
and a fragmentation into splintered
multiple identities, none secure.

And what of the world as seen by my father,
afflicted with a relentless sickness
since I was two years old, so I took for
granted that we weren't allowed to hug him,
that painful daily needles would appear,
that racking coughing fits could be heard through
bedroom walls, so early on I built up
a nervous hopefulness, the alternative
being too much to contemplate? What of
the devastation he must have gone through,
not just the disappointments of lost health,
but concern for our well-being taking
a toll of any remaining happiness?
Such an epitome of courage was
my mother that, in spite of everything,
I remember little but echoing
laughter, forward-lookingness, and hope.
If I think of the date I probably
was conceived, give or take a day or two,
it was during the most perilous time
of World War II, the Battle of Britain,
during the sunny days of September
nineteen forty, when Churchill's famous few
fought back the veritable armada
of German planes, that but for a rolling
dice in our favour, I could have been born
into a world deprived of any hope,
Hitler's legions strutting around Britain
and hardly likely to leave the misty
island to the west unmolested,
our neutrality scarcely a defence
against the murderousness of conquest.

My cousin Kevin made a famous film
about the Nazis taking up abode
in conquered Britain, so he obviously
had collywobbles thinking of such things.

Back from school for Easter, fifty-seven,
County Wicklow at its enticing best,
the grey Ferguson tractor making straight
furrows through the ten-acre field, I ran
up next morning to let Peter give me
the wheel since today would be harrowing,
not as difficult as ploughing or sowing
for my illicit driving skills. Jim had
the main gardens and kitchen garden
raked, weeded, spring flowers set off like jewels
against the green. My father had died a year
before, so this beloved place could not
go on indefinitely, besides I
was starting at Trinity in two years' time,
when we would need to move to the city.

The Italian word for room is *stanza*,
so a house made up of separate rooms
is akin to a poem, a construct
in which each unit tells its own story:
a fully realized poem or house
is much more than an aggregate of parts,
becomes its own sheltering haven.
Remembering my childhood homes, I see
my mother in many rooms, her talent
for making any space agreeable,
not just in a trivial sense of comfort,
but congruent with an endearing sense
of soul-enriching intimacy.

There was a fire grate in every room
at Ballanagh, even in the bedrooms,

but most grates had not been used for decades,
so going to bed involved rituals
of hugging rugs and hot-water bottles,
smells of rubber and hot steam, simmering
kettles on the Aga cooker all day.
A tribe of cats, both young and old, stretched out
along the wide Aga, the white cat Bán,
named after Pangur Bán in a Celtic
poem, would sleep happily on all the others.

There was a little room off the kitchen,
where my mother brought cut garden flowers
to make arrangements for the dining-room,
nearly always adorned for family,
and reception rooms when guests were coming;
this subtle art took her mind off graver
matters in a life of Snakes and Ladders,
(that game we played as children said it all).

What made those days so magical? Not just
that we had the glow of youth, energy,
and the joy that comes from constant newness
of experience, but the certainty
of love, solidarity of feeling,
courage and contentment and confidence
that life was supremely worth enjoying
in spite of tragedy, setbacks, self-doubt,
inevitable pain and dereliction.
There were times the sense of happiness
was so intense, I could hardly catch breath,
centrifugal waves of well-being
floating out to various imagined
horizons, setting up expectations
impossible to fulfil, so payback
time took a stringent toll on my feelings
as life made its periodic dips
into disintegration, requiring
a more-than-stoic stiff-upper-lipness.

When Memory Speaks

I vividly remember Shirley's
wedding, September nineteen fifty-five,
great friends and neighbours from the Baily days,
greeted on the road by Leo: "Hello,
Tim, are you going to the wedding?"
We had left the Baily two years earlier,
so it was lovely to see my postman
friend again. At that point, I had not lost
anyone to the otherworld, father
departing the following spring, first in
a roll call of too much loss, the only
mercy being it was spread out over time,
the human frame too fragile to take much
emptiness all at once, so one trains one's
self to bear absence with Hamlet's "absent
thee from felicity awhile" making
it all bearable. Do I believe in
happiness? Of course. However, it is
the offshoot of meaningful activity,
not something tangible to chase or seek—
as if it were a deer in hunter's sights,
relentlessly pursued— but elusive,
disappearing, water into water.

I had a special feeling for old maps,
Housman's "coloured counties", intuiting
the sounds and smells of each shire and township—
a book I had showed the English shires in colour:
Norfolk, Suffolk, Essex, and so on—
but I also did the same for my own
country, whose memories were more engrained:
I knew the feel of Waterford, Carlow,
Tipperary, Meath, Westmeath, Kildare,
as if I were a revenant coming
back from more than nine cats' lives, above all
I knew by heart the tactility of
County Wicklow—had I not walked its smooth-

curving hills, heathery slopes, its lonely
beaches where I swam one October
with my mother in the endless summer
of nineteen fifty-nine—had I not
bicycled hundreds of miles on twisting
country roads, on one occasion begging
a bed in the local police station,
on another a pause to chat with farmers
who were eager to be sent "shapes" from my snaps?
Had I not discovered literature
as I moved from the usual adolescent
fare to the bracing truthfulness of Jane
Austen, relished sentence by sentence
lolled on a deck-chair as I recovered
from the rigours of term-time at my school,
anticipating my going up to
Trinity, a new and unknown chapter?

III

65 Wellington Road, Ballsbridge, Dublin 4

At Trinity, relatively freelance
in my time-keeping after my rule-bound
schools, I took to designing each day
on blue index cards, the kind professors
would recommend for serious research
and keeping bibliographies and lists;
it became a lifelong habit, steering
my scattering thoughts into some semblance
of the straight and narrow path requisite
for success in academic work, indeed
for any other kind of achievement.
How sure and headstrong other people seemed
in their pursuit of success and money;
they seemed to know from the get-go just where
that distant goalpost was that drove them on.
How different was my sense of progress,
more like two steps back for every firm step
in a forward-facing orientation,
perhaps because I sensed more nuances
in every choice, and therefore agonized
over the most trivial decisions,
as if they were an eternal commitment—
how right I was: we are the sum total
of our decisions, great and small, never
free from the feeling that other choices
lead for ever into might-have-been lands.
So, when generations of students laugh
at my blue cards stacked in front of my desk,
full of ticks and crossings-out, I warn them
that I never had a built-in clockwork
certainty of where to put one foot
in front of another, so laugh they may,
but I know the anchors of my own ship.

Here, lurking in a drawer, I locate
a nineteen-sixty diary, open it
warily, not expecting much stirring

of the bones, much quiver of remorse.
March the tenth, I sang in the B Minor
Mass in Trinity; then a bicycle trip
to County Down to visit Saint Patrick's
grave for Saint Patrick's Day, innocent
at the border of future disorder
and hatred, a return to a past thought
safely dead and gone; news full of shootings
in Sharpeville, South Africa; when I returned
I published a lament for the numerous
dead: such atrocities were still abroad.
March the thirtieth, a simple entry:
"FIRST POEM", in bold print, embarking on
a lifetime of poetic involvement,
much to the dismay of my family.
Hard to evaluate the long impact
of such a quiet launching, an earnest
experiment in stilling the passing
moment, even then accelerating
too fast for comfort or comprehension.

So many people offering advice,
admonitions, warnings, prohibitions,
that often one walked with dizzying head
through air thickened with insecurity,
clouds of unknowing, fears of dereliction,
wondering how one was ever going
to emerge full-fledged from the miasma
of growing up, one's aims and ambitions
desperate for direction—stunned by grief
at my father's early death, I later
realized how all my faculties had
been orphaned, never finding older males
any help, perhaps I was too strange
a being, too introspective, quiet,
finding it hard to place myself in synch

with my contemporaries, seemingly
superior, yet inwardly ashamed—
I know not why—at my uniqueness,
knowing everyone else to be unique
but seeming too smug in their uniqueness
because backed up by some collective prop
I seemed to lack, always feeling alone.

I saw a play a week in my first year
at Trinity, so adjacently placed
at the hub of a city storied with
tales of writers, wits, poets, dramatists,
the roll-call of names embarrassingly
rich, *un embarras de richesse* indeed.
I never got tired of the habitual
summoning of Burke and Goldsmith, Berkeley
and Swift, the divine Oscar, bleak Beckett,
as I watched the buildings move about me;
Yeats was touted for a Professorship,
never made the cut, no academic
institution would long put up with him.
Thus the very stones prated of the where-
abouts of writers hard to live up to.
Joyce went to the other place: UCD,
things being divided then along strict lines,
a womb-to-tomb subtle segregation.
Catholic bishops taught their acolytes
that walking in the gates of Trinity
was akin to a mortal sin; many,
however, defied such antiquations,
among them merry Brendan Kennelly,
poet and encourager of poets,
silver-tongued lecturer and Yeatsian;
tough-minded Eavan Boland, intent on
forging a code for the hidden Ireland
of dispossession and lonely voices.

Why all this emphasis on works of art?
Is it a blessing or a curse to see
the world continually magnified
or minimized by great art, music, words?
At first, it seemed an easy channelling
of emotion to share with other minds,
but sad experience convinces one
that fellow feeling of this kind is rare,
that people are more likely to be puzzled
or downright hostile, misunderstanding
one's love for snobbery, arty-craftiness,
and rejection of the ordinary business
of society. My early passion
for Yeats, for example, evinced remarks
not meant to hurt, but said with serious
moral earnestness: "Poetry will get
you nowhere fast," rational advice
that certainly had a point, but damping
one's enthusiasm for the present.
All too easy to become an effete
rejector of the common way of life,
to disdain all feeling but the rarest,
as if life were a French Impressionist
painting or a poem by Mallarmé.

But after a while one learns to become
stoic and self-possessed, knowing that most
callings are lonely, long explorations
of a grassy, rocky road not travelled
by anyone before or after, just
you alone with the terrifying fate
to be yourself, no matter what the cost.
Yeats himself, already a famous man,
had paused on the stairway of his tower,
stilled by a sudden doubt in his own life
and work, regretting the easy commerce
of relationships another life seemed

to promise, and wondering what price
the ruthless gods of art had exacted.
Enough, there is no room for doubt, no room
for thinking too precisely on the event,
for thinking is the enemy of art,
not that art is thoughtless, but it must strike
with all the mental irons in the fire
and seem forged in supra-rational flames
of fusion, synthesis, and mystery.

And then there is the question of the self;
for most people, lyric poetry
is merely self-exposure, the first-person
"I" just an excuse to put oneself first.
But there are so many "I's", each moment
of one's life is potentially unique
in its perceptions and expression, self
cart-wheeling, shape-changing into multi-
faceted entities, each one a probe
into futures never glimpsed until then.
Above all, art is never just selfish,
provided that it transcends the ego,
and catches something of the higher Self
talked of by Jung and others, the whole sphere
rather than a segment or slice of life,
or an earth-shot taken from the moon
as the early astronauts just gasped
at the beauty of the suspended earth
from a distance never seen before:
so is the Self seen from one's inner space.

Art shows us that we are not alone,
that knowledge may be fragmentary
but that feeling is primordial,
linking us to generations before
and to those unborn, an essential link
in the chain of being, without which no

satisfactory existence can thrive.
One learns as one goes along that people
are not so scared of the usual things
as they are of being caught out by feeling,
a constant vigil on the emotions—
as not to be seen crying in public—
yet proving by one's stoic stance that one
does have feeling, kept rigidly in control.
So my favourite mode of art or life
is a blend of formal, informal modes,
smart without being smartypants, casual
without going off the rails, behaviour
both dignified and nonchalant, trial
and error taken in stride, so constant
is one's inner compass pointing true north
and all points around the whirling spectrum.

Close heat of a Parisian July,
a rooftop view of chimneys and red slates;
Jill brought me a bunch of flowers. Later
we quarrelled, and the flowers went fluttering
down, shattering the Chagall illusion
of the perfect lovers in their skyscape.

Jill's rented car had a rattling hubcap—
a bolt got stuck inside it, so cobbled
streets along the Seine come reassembled
as if my mind had minimized the scene
for future recall—we drove to Harfleur
in Normandy, an old-fashioned seaside
town frequented by painters—memories
of seascapes by Boudin, Monet, spanking
flags flapping briskly in the salty air.
On Bastille Day, we mingled with the crowds
along the Seine, explosions of fireworks
for hours into the night. I was reading
for exams, such books as Matthew Arnold's

Culture and Anarchy, with its Philistines
and "sweetness and light", a touching tribute
to an era whose iconography
still echoed powerfully for lone minds
such as mine, seeking to find a balance
between modernity and things long past.

So one builds up the person that one is,
the faults and flaws as important as the rest,
for they provide the background dark against
which one can struggle to foil entropy,
the endless deterioration
of one's faculties a ceaseless challenge,
making the more exhilarating
those rarest moments of redemption,
of glimpses into beauty, truth, meaning,
so that one knows that they exist, but can't
explain how or why one believes, because
beauty grasped is no longer beauty,
but a twittering bird in a mental cage.

I never considered another job
but that of teaching, so the more I learned,
the more I could impart. Information
is just the groundwork, anyone can grasp
percentages, lists, dates, names, opinions,
but at what point does mere information
become firm knowledge, let alone wisdom?
Something to do with beginning to see patterns,
trends, swerves in history; structure in art;
narrative flow in literature; meaning
in philosophy; precision in speech;
pragmatic results in science. What were
my priorities that I wanted to
convey, the essential baton I wished
to pass on, lest the race be vain,
or just stumbling from day to dreary day?

Priority number one: poetry
as conceived by Shelley, Blake, Keats, and Yeats—
yes, that is Keets and Yates, not Kates and Yeets—
a high-flown Romantic conception, sure,
but also an art of the possible.
Poetry not just as literary art,
but also suffusing life like
yeast (another way of spelling Yeats), seed
of all true inspiration, for it is
fuelled by that same pattern-sensing power
that creates knowledge out of information.

Above all, a refusal to dislodge
art from life, for they interpenetrate
each other like fine strands of DNA:
a defiance in the face of all glum
expositors of Gradgrind facts, dreary
theorizers who want to fit all things
into a pre-conceived architecture
of thought, ignoring intuition, dream,
the infinite twist of form in finite
creation, the individualizing
tendency of nature as it explores
the best possible manifestations
of the world-soul. "OK, my dear savant,
this is fair enough for the higher modes
of abstract thought, but we like to stay
a step or two ahead of the boys, who
will never guess at our ineptitude."
O yes, they will, to teach anything from
the basics up, you need to know the whole
exfoliation of the field, to have
a dignified humility in the face
of the implicit complicatedness
of the simplest word, the simplest concept,
so you can truly say "I do not know,"
but never, "Who cares about these textures

and more-than-nautical knots of being
and unbeing?" Was this a vain belief?

Teaching is like gardening, too much loss
of potential, faith, looking-forwardness
can cripple one at times, yet next morning
a perfect blossom shows unexpected
hope in the continuity of things.
So each triumph is dearly paid for in
yearly bonfires of autumnal leaves,
and happiness forever elusive
the more one chases it. The best results
are to be had by paying attention
to each particular, by focusing
the teeming bustle of reality
into a spot of burning light, and so
create a microcosm of detail.
The best thing you can teach is that success
is always earned in tiny increments,
so start small, and work steadily outwards
from a shining centre, the infinite
surmised in expanding rippling waves
of comprehension. Inch forward in miles.

So it is with reading. A nine-hundred-
page novel is made up of words, lines, strokes
of punctuation, gaining its effect
only in time, like music, each sentence
or phrase, melody or cadence, slow drops
in the bucket of the whole, visibly
increasing in volume only slyly,
like the imprint of each moment on one's
consciousness, here and gone so slidingly
it is hard to say, is this now myself
or but a fleeting shadow on the wall
of passing phenomena, like sooty
city walls as one slows into stations

in a train, and is the arrival point
an arrival at anything except
another transition to the unknown?

As for poetry, what is the point of it?
Ah, if I could answer that I could fly,
apt parallel perhaps, for poetry
negates our usual gravity-prone
experience, giving us potential
wings—"O for the wings of a dove"—lifting
us into flightiness of metaphor
and into the weight-defying power
of symbol, so that the curved horizon
becomes a luminous accomplishment
of our longing. But this is not escape,
for true poetry must have a weight, tilt
the scale of truth towards enlightenment.
Each poem is therefore a grain of salt
on the weighing scales of deeper meaning,
an act of attention that drives chaos
away by its habit of hanging out.

See how long you can go with one word at
a time, line by line, word by word, ten taps
per line as you count the beat of each sound
as they fall like flakes of snow, flake by flake,
snow on snow, drift on drift, the bulk and growth
of mass, of heft, of thought, the weight of pins
grown to tons—such is our life as we live
from day to day, breath by breath, smile by smile,
to build our dreams, our souls, our fates:
such accumulation, inheritance.

William Cecil, Lord Burghley, once queried
Queen Elizabeth: "All this for a song?"
His bureaucratic mind objected to
a mere poet (Spenser) being paid cash

for paltry verse (*The Faerie Queene* no less).
He had no qualms about feathering his
own little nest, the massive Burghley House,
whose rooftop outlines the sky like a town.

Bedtime ritual of banana, glass
of milk, and something to read: a hardback
copy of Wordsworth's *Prelude*, a woodcut
of "The Stolen Boat" on the dust-jacket
surrounded by the deepest Chagall blue.
Finals were in September; these April rites
helped calm my nerves, imprinting a ghostly
braille of rhythm on my expanding mind.

Thus the long spring of nineteen sixty-three,
reading that stubborn and austere young man,
I explored the growth of his poetic mind—
something I was hoping for in myself—
I knew it takes a lifetime's attention,
and that every second counts, even those
that are invisible and fleeting—
"No act of attention is ever lost,"
wrote the great Simone Weil, a major mind
I discovered later in my twenties,
a young schoolmaster, striving to impart
the rudiments with my scratchy knowledge.
Why was my mind different?: something to do
with the way it butterflied from one thing
to another with no apparent logic,
controlled only by my inner daimon.
To render things into sequential prose
always seemed to me a dragging down,
a reduction to what is called "prosaic",
or rather a *reductio ad absurdum,*
yet the poetic realm held equal dangers
of letting go too soon, perhaps too late.
"Some burn damp faggots," wrote W.B.,

that daunting master of the longest view,
who yet made music out of every dark
setback and wrong turning in his youth;
he saw the whole trajectory as one
long, high, singing arrow-shot of longing
sent into the fibrous dream-laden air,
maybe landing out of sight and mind
or else bearing fruit in yet unborn minds
of others doing mental piggy-backs
on his paper-piercing acts of attention.

Perhaps the Irish are very right-brained—
that would explain much of the method in
their madness, or madness in their method.
Since Bacon and Newton, as William Blake
knew, the Saxon mind wants clear-cut answers,
but poetry needs to be implicit:
perhaps this is why England has produced
so many poets and great actors, as
antidote to the general pressure-
cooker feeling of keep-it-all-in-check.
In Dublin, with much more soft tolerance
for eloquence, too many novelists
and poets talk and drink their lives away:
no wonder Beckett, Wilde, Yeats, and Shaw,
let alone Joyce, had to test their logos-
driven brains in foreign climes, the shocking
anonymity of Trieste, Zürich,
the making of Joyce, the French Resistance
enabling Beckett's absurdity,
his Shakespearean sense of life as dream,
as stage, as leaving not a rack behind.
What would Shaw be without London critics,
or Yeats without the Cheshire Cheese on Fleet
Street, or penniless visits to Paris?

How was I to orchestrate my slipshod,

turbulent, contradictory feelings
not just for today but for a lifetime?
Such thoughts made me weak with apprehension
rather like Keats's "teasing out of thought
as doth eternity"; somehow one must
get through the day, the morrow, and so on
without going off the rails, but steady,
steady rhythmic progress along the lines
laid out by family, tradition, while
keeping personal dreams, lusts, and fears
within all reasonable boundaries.

"What are you going to be when you grow up?"
career advisors would boringly ask:
train-driver (just kidding), solicitor,
navy, army, air force candidate, British
of course; such possibilities were not
just remote, they were hilarious
to contemplate, by the time I'd sorted
out the political complexities.
So what was my heritage and background?—
a mongrel Huguenot, Anglo, Celtic,
French mix, a temperament made for times
not our own, a body very glad for
modern surgery, my legs broken by
a surgeon when I was born—to keep them straight.

Most of my contemporaries were off
to Swinging London or points farther afield,
but I was stubbornly attached to home.
I knew early on the UK was not
for me, although I loved traditional
English ways, in a Betjemanesque way—
don't get me wrong, no sycophant
or time-server, but I loved the odour
of ancient buildings, damp country houses,
cathedrals, capacious armchairs in clubs

which friends sometimes invited me into,
the leather creaking like old men's knee-joints
as one lowered into them. I relished
the English poetic voice, above all
the whole Romantic nineteenth century,
which seemed so close, a century later,
to my own Irish delayed upbringing
with its aching landscapes of hopeless hope,
its unfulfilled dreams, its vague sexlessness,
its horrified awareness of Nature
as a cruel, unforgiving mistress,
its spoiled lyricism, like a wasp-sting
at a picnic—all this taught me that life
was a mirage that deluded even
the wise, the beautiful, the circumspect,
but worst of all, those who refused to plunge
into the tide, and gamble their chances
on a fortuitous sleight-of-fate.

So when in that graduating summer
an ad appeared with my old school wanting
an assistant master, French and German,
English, lots of freelance amateur
umpiring, refereeing, supervising,
I gave it a whirl, although misgivings
at once set in, as I dreaded becoming
a Mr. Chips, beloved by all, but stuck
for life in those potentially awful
institutions, boarding schools. The wretched
loneliness of the buildings I learned to
hate the minute the boys (no girls in sight)
left to go home for the holidays. Blank
fear took hold of me—would I be still here
with no escape until I was sixty?
But my salvation was I was a sly
rebel— directing several major plays
with a passion, Hamlet's "the play's the thing/

to catch the conscience of the King" in mind.
Sure enough, after that, drama took on
more weight in bureaucratic minds, who up
till then thought it a mere interruption
of the serious stuff of schooling: Maths,
Latin, and perhaps History, given
pride of place. I sympathized instinctively
with youth (was I not a youngster, too?)
and made friends for life among the pupils.
But although I knew I wanted to teach,
I knew that this was not the place or time
to lay down roots. I needed change, money,
and a new horizon to find myself.

A perfect June afternoon in early days
as a schoolmaster, my task to umpire
the third-eleven cricket match, lazy
post-prandial time-consumer, laundered
whites as pupils bowled and batted, flashes
of attention as a bowler twisted
around and shouted "Howsatt?" God forbid
if I were dozing or day-dreaming, tuned
in to the floating invisible song
of the cuckoo as it threaded the air
of subtle-curved Kilmashogue, the mountain
above the school grounds, merging into Synge
country, where he walked with his dog, Ben,
meeting tramps and cottagers, sounding out
those haunting cadences some call Synge-song;
but those who know the region can only
admire, so accurately he caught the tone,
the cadence, the melancholy, the lilt
of mountainy men and women, only
ten miles from Dublin, but might as well be
in *L'Irlande profonde* of Connemara
or West Kerry, or the Mayo back-roads.

After a break for tea, the match resumed,
that cuckoo (or was it more than one?)
in another part of the taut canvas
of the afternoon as it faded into
early summer evening, drifting scents
of hay-ricks and recently cut long grass
keeping my memory on its toes
until challenged again to arbitrate
a leg-before-wicket decision, tough
call as one had to gauge the flightiness
of the ball as it bounced, spun, and slight-grazed
the batsman's padded legs—before replay
technology a difficult gut-feel,
especially if one were really away
with the fairies, led on by misleading
cuckoos mapping out the soundscape above.
A student met forty years later
remembered a dreamy colleague of mine
caught napping, whereupon the poor boy was
out, although the ball was in fact a wide.
Such ecstasies of laughter we had then.

Samuel Beckett played first-class cricket
for the Trinity team, legendary
players among them. Beckett is the sole
Nobel prizewinner to have an entry
also in *Wisden*, the cricketers' bible.
You remember one of Beckett's bitter
old protagonists, the monologist
in *Molloy*, and his interminable,
wry meditation on absurdity,
as he shifted six pebbles from one pocket
to another, having slow-sucked them all.
Beckett knew very well that the umpire
in a cricket game often kept six stones,
or pebbles, in his capacious white coat.
As the bowler loosed each ball down the pitch,

the umpire moved another smooth pebble
to the opposite pocket so he kept
an accurate tally of the balls (six
per over), and not make a balls of it.
Absurdity or real-life conundrum?
It was all a tinker's curse to Molloy:
play up and play the game in Irish style.

I had a bed-sitting room overlooking
the deer park and the Hurley Lane winding
up to the furzy slopes of Kilmashogue.
A busy stream came to a holding tank
outside the window, then plunged underground,
emerging two hundred yards down the school
property beside the music rooms, where
its channeled gurglings often beguiled me.
I was an assistant master, at first just
four years older than the senior boys,
but soon learning what a sad profession
schoolmastering is, young generations
changing so quickly, one feels quite ancient
by the age of thirty. But we were young,
could cope with many disappointments,
meanwhile leaving enough blue sky to catch
the joys as they flew.

                    Michael, who became
a distinguished sculptor, remembers
the faded yellowish dust-jacket
of a book by my bedside table, Clare's
The Shepherd's Calendar, and compares it
to the colour of the college gatelodge—
such the butterfly quirks of memory.
When I later had the hard dilemma
of emigrating to build my career,
knowing I could never reconnect with
what I deeply loved in my own country,

that bedside book came floating from my deep brain
guiding me to irreversible paths
once dreamed of as I read myself to sleep:
thus, everything one reads is always there.

Never good in the mornings, duty day
was a trial of discipline—up at
six-thirty, presiding over breakfast—
that hushed cacophony of cutlery
and bleary greetings; stand up straight to say
the Latin grace, be-gowned: mischievous boys
longing for one's mistakes, ineptitudes.
Those early mornings were a joy in May,
the bare trees acquiring a sudden sheen,
dawn bird-heralded. I'd sit on the front steps
of the Georgian house and pan over
the curve of Dublin Bay, that "swerve of shore,"
Howth peninsula with its hump-backed outline
sending back bitter-sweet admonishments.

It's strange how, looking back, things seem so clear,
as if ordained from time immemorial,
making one forget the angst, the sweating
cold and hot at 2:00 a.m., the nervous
dipping of mental toes in possible scenarios,
the heady or scary "What-if"s and "No-
no"s—my remedy was a cup of tea,
and as much music as I could stand—
what would I have done before long-players,
stereo recordings coming in just
as I graduated—the Brandenburgs
heard in multiple layers through earphones
were more than enough to keep me off drugs?
No special virtue, just a bit of luck
that music was my aphrodisiac,
and to a lesser extent, poetry.

Before I graduated, another trip to France
was desirable, to polish up my
spoken French. I found myself in Bordeaux
where cousins of former neighbours welcomed
me to their affluent town house, and then
to a summer place at Arcachon, pine
needle-scented, miles and miles of sand-dunes.
"L'été n'est qu'un rêve en Irlande," I told
my hosts, as the sun melted and dispersed
my Northern negation of the body.
The joy of being fully fit, sniffing
the scent of new tennis balls and taut cat-
gut on one's racquet, mown grass and perfume
and healthy sweating bodies, as one swung
and smacked a bull's-eye return on match point.

Swimming the rocky shallows of Le Gard
as it gurgled under the massive arches
of Le Pont du Gard, greatest of all Roman
aqueducts: inclination, gentle flow
of water drawn from ancient hidden springs,
water below, and criss-crossing above.
Water, water everywhere, *fons et
origo*, stuff of life, that into which
we cannot step twice, if once, mystery
of this fluid becoming ice, fog, steam,
that ebbs and flows through landscapes like bloodlines
through the body.

                        Chugging along on my
mobylette, a mere bicycle with power,
exposed to every changing sensation
as I moved from strong sun into a long
mountain tunnel, froze, then out into sun,
I travelled from Grenoble through the French
Alps down to Avignon, at one pit-stop
trading a copy of *Madame Bovary*

I was reading for an overnight kip.
From Avignon, I aimed at Paris, stopped
for a week in Beaujolais to labour
in the vineyards, dawn to dusk, with robust
farm meals provided along with stipend,
and a friendly farmer's dog called Moustique.
In Paris, I inadvertently went
the wrong way down a one-way street: klaxons
blared as a sinister-looking police
van known as a Black Maria pulled up
in front of me; bike and self were without
further ado turfed into the van, brought
to a nearby station and put behind bars—
no stout *garda* or friendly *bobby* here.

On another trip to France, in Bordeaux,
a fellow guest in my *pension*
asked me to drive him round famous vineyards
since he was training for a New York house
and needed to concentrate on his trade.
His calling card opened up some wonders:
a cellar tour of Château Lafite-Rothschild
and lunch at Château Lascombes, eight tasting glasses
perched at each setting (just a mouthful each
in case you were thinking of the driving).
To this day, the names of that storied region
float in and out of my filing desk mind:
Saint Médard-en-Jalles I seem to recall
for no reason—its Proustian lilt enough
to set my impressionable nerve-ends going.
I did once fancy myself as a wine-
taster in training, but such things needed
family capital to go beyond dreams,
so I returned to my quiet bookish
life, staving off disappointment for now.

Although English and Irish literature
took over from French during my career,
La France profonde remained a litmus test
of the civilized life, in spite of rude
waiters, shouting taxi drivers, and sour
landladies: I remember Kenneth Clark
standing on the Pont Neuf, and gesturing
towards the Îsle de la Cité, with its
ancient profile, including Notre Dame
de Paris, recently almost destroyed,
another treasure gone from what he called
Civilisation, that thunderous word.
No one can define it, but why not try
to grasp the capacious depth of homage
that we owe to events and characters
that managed to evade the ravenous
open jaws of history, like the grotesque
sculptures in the wild Italian garden,
Bomarzo? Was mine the last generation
to feel history on its fingertips,
to know it as an abattoir, and yet
so grateful for anything that squeaked through?
All I know is that I treasure my own
development as a kind of victory
over constantly encroaching darkness,
whether of the mind, or body, or soul,
each poem a little shoot of spring-time
transferred to words, and, one hopes, to hearts.
For human beings are at their best
when in transcendence, nothing mystical,
but caught in the filigree of action,
as in sports, or stilled by meditation,
as in the timeless timeliness of art.

Such things made up the good life for the time
being, before the shades of the prison
house began to close in, and the long twilight

of youth glimmered on the horizon.
Thank heavens for the strict austerity
of those boarding schools I later taught at,
it kept me wary of the unzipping
of the flies that was the Swinging Sixties,
but posed a problem for a youth in thrall
to too much inner contemplation
rather than a whole-bodied immersion
in the *Zeitgeist*. Family, Fatherland,
and Faith, all had their Joycean nets
to entangle their victims like ghost-gear,
and tying you up in obligation
before you knew what was happening
and mapping out an alien future
one had little aptitude or zeal for.

IV

No Fixed Abode

So the negotiations of growing up,
reluctant to jettison innocence
yet well aware that maturity drives
one onward into the unknown, each day
an experiment in living as well
as inheritance, character, and fate
allow, not forgetting the vagaries
of intimates and friends, always pushing
one into scenarios of their own
invention.
          And sometimes something rougher,
more unexpected, more deeply painful,
as on the wet November evening
I called at my sister's house, until then
a haven of normal family life:
"Have you heard about our brother Christopher?"—
the first sharp stab of family failure,
the first moral shock that drove me inwards
to find stability in a sour,
disintegrating youth, when all my dreams
rose up like mocking harridans, to prod
and poke and twist my feelings into shreds,
a sense of falling backwards into deep
meaninglessness, my moral fibre stretched
to breaking point, glad of having had tough
practice in the often arcane rituals
of school, a sense that one could keep going.

In short, the family business father
had courageously built up through the drab
thirties, had suddenly vanished, Harold
Wilson having unexpectedly
devalued the pound, sinking my brother's
over-risky recent investment.
It was a time of rancour, blame, and spleen,
of never-to-be-forgotten arguments,
accusations, wringing of hands, if not

actual necks, of a deepening sense
of self-laceration at one's former
enthusiasms, some of which seemed just
vanity of middle-class vanities—
"what now?" sang Plato's ghost. I had no answer,
no firm footing in family, nation,
employment, thrown back on my inner self,
putting it to the ultimate trial:
what was I good for? What does it all mean?

I out-hamleted Hamlet in questions,
in self-loathing, surpassed Swift in railing
against the basics of humanity,
finding Beckett suddenly relevant
in his forecast of absolute zero:
I seemed to move forward, if forward
it was, in a state of fundamental
numbness, the springs of creativity
iced over, clogged up, the former pathways
of the mind strewn with debris, sharp-stinging,
face-lashing branches. But worst of all
was the loss of my inner compass-point,
the inborn sense of high aspiration
toward goals both near and far, a conviction
that life was an earnest exploration
of forever-deepening wisdom.

"There are in our existence spots of time"—
it was Wordsworth's disappointment and dismay
and his coming to terms with it that proved
my own salvation, that model of harsh
self-knowledge tempered by self-discipline,
an awareness of the poet's temper,
one given to wild swings of deep feeling,
feelings that normal people seemingly
could master or at least dissimulate.
Was it possible to be a poet

after plumbing such turbulent, murky
waters; after such knowledge, what forgiveness?
Renovation began the moment I
discovered that the family romance
I had nurtured was a path to hard light
as well as darkness, that, like Coleridge's
Mariner, I began to heal when I
inadvertently found blessings in harsh
realities, read the Stoic writers,
learned Marcus Aurelius by heart,
to be mouthed and mumbled through snow and sleet.

Had I not my health? My mind? My stringent
upbringing to bind into my outlook,
which had to be optimistic, or what
would have become of me? Those who slouched
around complaining about trivial
things I had to extrude forcibly
from my environment, as they could drag
me down, the fall so swift, the clambering
up laborious and time-intensive.
Like saints with evil: "Get thee behind me,"
I would repeat like a mantra, to banish
any waste of breath, of space, of time,
Transcendental Meditation coming
further to my rescue, eliminating
pointlessness, relaxing me into
weightlessness of being, lightness of mind.

No matter how endowed with good fortune
one is, times of severe setback make one
a philosophical ruminant, chewing
on the same sour grass interminably,
and the danger arises of getting
mud-locked in a permanent despair,
not helped by too much reading in the swamp
of nineteenth-century morbid decadence.

Much as I love Baudelaire and Wilde,
Verlaine, Mallarmé, Rimbaud and the rest,
I strive to open windows on fresher
winds, and more expansive intimations
of meaning, finding in the arch-poet
Yeats a serene, long-term sublimation
of my inner conflicts; closer to home,
indeed, he came with all the tragic load
of history, his verse a Jungian
exercise in transcending bitterness,
a common pitfall of the Irish fate,
a coping with irreconcilables:
the rift started by the Reformation
lasted, to my chagrin, into modern
times, disguised in the Republic of Ireland by soft
plasterings of velvety speech, but cracks
lurked underneath nonetheless, revealing
themselves in unexpected dagger-stabs
of maliciousness, anger, or deceit,
every conviction hard-won in youth
turned upside-down, such topsy-turvydom
a norm in one's mature years, history
coming home to roost in one's own backyard.

Easter nineteen seventy, I drove back
from the South of France to London after
some months of self-examination.
I found myself in Paris on Good Friday,
so I tentatively entered Notre Dame—
being a Huguenot by descent,
a committed Anglican by nurture—
and exposed my troubled mind and conscience
to the beauty of the ritual,
the majesty of the ancient building,
the impeccable French of the service:
"Seigneur, Tu sais tout, Tu sais que je T'aime,"
intoned the priest, and I was riveted

with that vague longing for traditional
"sanctity and loveliness" that Shakespeare
must have felt when he saw the whitewashing
of the church walls over the old frescoes,
decapitation of Virgin Mary
statues, and the iconoclastic rage
that smashed so much that had seemed so sacred
"where late the sweet birds sang." Poets ever since
have felt this tug-of-war within their art,
a fierce nostalgia for unity
of thought and action, for wholeheartedness,
undividedness, seamless sympathy
between body, mind and soul, the instincts
and the reason reasonably infused,
what Keats meant by a vale of soul-making,
Dante rejoicing in nature's abundance
but lamenting its often trembling hand.

Having crossed the Channel on the ferry,
I drove through Canterbury the next day—
Easter Saturday—attended evensong
at the cathedral, with its enormous naves,
paid my respects at Thomas à Becket's
tomb, rejoiced in the equilibrium
that Anglican services embody,
thanks, historians say, to the first Queen
Elizabeth, who held a balance between
extremes of Puritan and Catholic,
a model, surely, for everyday life,
at least one I try to emulate.

Then on to London, Westminster Abbey
glowing in early morning light, my mother,
who bequeathed to me her poetic soul,
pointing out memorials to poets,
the slender Waterford glass chandeliers,
deep relishing the medieval bells

as we toured Poets' Corner afterwards—
Chaucer's tomb, Eliot, "O rare Ben Jonson"—
the organ fugue reaching consummation.
I wondered afterwards how many times
this peregrination had been achieved:
three cities, three shrines, two divergent faiths
whose ramifications have so altered,
poisoned the wells of my inheritance.

On my way out to France, at lowest
mental ebb, the forces of my spirit
stretched out in arid, long panoramas
of dry sand, I revisited Cambridge,
that ancient fount of English poetry—
dating from Chaucer at Trumpington Street—
a friend put me in a guest room at King's,
where E.M. Forster was at High Table.
I attended several evensongs
in Chapel, overjoyed that the singing
that week concentrated on William Byrd,
for me a high point, not just of English,
but of European music, his Mass
In Five Parts elegiacally healing
wounds both self-inflicted and otherwise,
my iced-over feelings shifting somewhat;
infelix ego: exactly my state of mind
as I yearned upwards to the fan vaulting,
polyphonies mounting to dying falls.

My frail bark shivered her creaking timbers,
as I thought of what I needed to confront,
my *piccioletta barca* heaving on
mounting waves of dread, and yet excitement—
Oh Beatrice dolce guida e cara!
How could any paradise be attained
without that longing leap after blockage?
"Was it for this?" I remembered Wordsworth's

fear that his astonishing, astonished
childhood would lead into banality,
or worse, coruscating guilt at talents
wasted, frittered, lost in self-deceptions.
He walked back along his childhood river,
so to speak, letting its soft abrasions
against rocks and weeds and sandy shallows
enter his two brains, not at loggerheads
for once, knowing all true achievement lets
the oppositions in one's nature fuse,
curing what had seemed irredeemable.

And what about my country? Did it not
at times deny my full belongingness,
citing deeply engrained historical
leftovers? Shaw once said that there were no
other skies like Irish skies, and my ilk
had absorbed those skiey influences
for hundreds of years, enough, one would think,
to prefer above all else the windy
deliciousness of crouching from a sudden
squall beneath seaside shrubbery, as waves
of noisy rain came and went, leaving one
shivering in renewed bursts of sunshine.
Are such feelings merely superficial?
I think not, but they hardly stack up when
the argument turns on political
affiliations and stern commitments,
and all the dreary accusations fuelled
by misunderstandings and history.
So emerged my deep belief that I was
a citizen of a broader country,
whose borders could unstoppably expand,
whose GNP was built up in the mind,
whose service was perfect freedom from hate
and mercenary Utopian lies.
Such citizenship I found in Irish

literature, in Gaelic if I could,
but mostly in the hybrid Hiberno-
English forged by centuries of rival,
yet complementary interlocutions
and attempts to outdo the other side
in eloquence, in cogency, in sure
coinage of the dialect of the tribe—
such cultural capital is solid
ground under one's feet, unlike the shifting
loyalties and misappropriations
of actual soil, soiled with too much death.

"When in disgrace with fortune and men's eyes"
I speed on my Harry Potter magic
imagination to lonely towers:
Yeats's, Jung's, Hölderlin's, perhaps above
all to Michel de Montaigne's retirement
château near Bordeaux, where he came to think
after serving as mayor of Bordeaux,
while sectarian wars were raging all
over Europe; here he converted each
storey of the round tower on the estate,
chapel on the ground floor, then his bedroom,
then his study, fifty-nine quotations
from the classics inscribed on the rafters,
so as he wrote those marvellous essays,
more like forays, shy explorations
into sceptical, indeed heretical
territory, he only had to glance
up from his writing to feel deep kinship
with the ancients: Terence, Ovid, Virgil,
Homer, Aristotle with his golden
mean, so much lacking in the world around.
*"Nous tous, les vivants, rien que fantômes,
Sans poids."* Thus Sophocles in French:
"We, the living, no more than weightless shades."
The chapel had a concave ceiling, starred

with painted heavens, the light of far stars
reaching him as he slept above, keeping
real nightmares at bay, and daymares in shape.
His humble conclusion from all this thought:
"Que sais-je?" What in heaven's name do I know?
Those who think they know are busy slitting
each other's throats in ecstatic vengeance
paid out to those who will not toe the line,
making sure that their enemies know what hell
is like, while we are on our way to bliss.

Why do modern artists, writers, thinkers
inevitably want to rub our nose
in degradation, as if to say: "Fool,
how dare you to be smug in such a world?"
As if now were quantitatively worse
than times when people were burnt in public,
limbs sawn off without any relief
of medicine, power was absolute, mostly
horrible in its secret detailing;
but great things have always been done in spite
of human cruelty and ignorance,
and to celebrate greatness is not to
turn one's back on suffering, it is to
enable one to meet adversity
with less indignity than otherwise.

For Emily Dickinson, poetry
was possibility, a fairer house
than prose, Schiller was inspired by the smell
of rotten apples, Addison and Byron
walked up and down a designated space—
gallery or cloister—a glass of wine
rewarding them at each turn of the plough.
Wordsworth paced up and down at Alfoxden
and the rough roads around Dove Cottage,
scaring the locals with his self-mumbling.

Even the clumsy Coleridge walked miles
to meet his belovèd Wordsworth, leaping
a gate in anticipation; Yeats slept
among the rhododendrons at Howth Castle,
and found secret caves below the cliff paths
that wind around the Howth peninsula.
Synge walked the Wicklow hills in all weathers,
inventing a syntax, unknown until then,
which caught local speech in a persistent
rhythm consistent as the falling rain
or the acrid smells of burnt gorse, or peat-
smoke drifting from the hearths of cottages,
nostrils dilated by ancient fibres.
Housman famously cut himself shaving
when he thought of a line of poetry,
Hardy used the barks of trees as manuscripts,
noticing the endless diversity
of commonplace phenomena, sadness
pervading him like a returning ghost.

What long walks I found in varied landscapes,
perambulations or mere sauntering,
ambling along content to discover
what lay around the next corner,
an exercise in anticipation,
a musical setting up of contexts
and landscaped syntax, as in the garden
at Stourhead, where the ups and downs the path
takes, the sudden glimpses of hidden views,
the circular goal, the meditations
along the way, give their own take on things,
philosophical, visceral at once,
the moment held in balance with deep time,
and insouciant as a musician
pitted against a complete orchestra
with a single solo intonation.
Above all, the joy of seeing without

being seen, that evolutionary
advantage that contributes to aesthetics,
interlocking prospects with retrospects,
the sense of being above and beyond
while also sniffing the drifting pollen.

Denis Diderot once described long walks
that he had taken with a friend, only
later divulging that they were dream-walks
inspired by the paintings of Vernet.
Renoir mentioned that he loved those paintings
that made him want to saunter within them.
My favourite painted walks are Pissarro's:
through the crowded streets of Rouen, the tiles
of the steep-angled gables pinky-red,
while above them the Gothic towers and spires
of the cathedral block out the pale sky,
one's eye like a sparrow at roof-top height.
Monet's poppy fields, women and children
enjoying childhood as it should be,
before the self-conceit of adulthood
robs nature of her proper modesty.
And what walks are better than Marcel Proust's,
where we recognize the territory
because it is imprinted on our nerves
since time immemorial, like those elms
that Tennyson heard animated by bees?

What are the enemies of poetry?
Money coats experience with varnish,
a pseudo-protective film, giving
the illusion that raucous life can be
kept at bay, or the worse delusion that
worldly goods equate to long-lasting good.
Shelley may have been an atheist,
but I must agree with milord Byron
when he said of his recently drowned

friend that everyone else was as a beast
in comparison, so quick-silvered was
his wit, his intellect, and just his soul.

Imagination cures slavish envy:
example, I always enjoy scanning
other people's houses in my mind's eye,
the grander the better, say a mini-
castle in Scotland, packed with turrets, steps
up and down and sideways; heavy rain pelts
on steep roofs and cone-shaped towers, making
the inmates nudge their deep armchairs closer
to the roaring, crackling fire. No matter
that this is just a dream, the unconscious
mind doesn't care which is which, thank heavens.
I've lived a thousand different lives in such
imaginary settings, giving me
little room for unnecessary angst.

V

302 Stong College, York University, Toronto, Ontario

Fifty years ago I was sharpening
my wits and damping down my emotions
as I packed (what to take?) for a new life
in Canada. Toronto, here I come,
as if it cared, but I did come trailing
references and contacts, if not
clouds of glory, at least recognition
for my labours on *The Dublin Magazine*.
My sister and her husband waved me off
at Dublin Airport, a quick hop to Shannon,
where I checked in, looked out the plate-glass
window: Jaysus, Brownlow, look at the size
of that fucking plane, it must be six times
what I'm used to. Long flight to Montreal,
where I registered as "Landed Immigrant",
then on to Toronto, horizon-to-
horizon concrete, the lights of traffic
snaking seemingly into infinity.
Time, Brownlow, to remember your p's and q's,
"get a grip," as an English college friend
used to say, this is indeed 'sink or skim,'
all values I had learned in my prolonged
childhood growth came into urgent play,
never having had a continuing
city, now is your chance to thrill or spill.

The minute I stepped on Canadian ground
I knew I had made the right decision:
the polite reply of "You're welcome"
fell on my starved ears as mellifluous,
tired with what Nan used to call "boothash",
a word peculiar to herself but true
to the abrasive interactions
of aggressive Irish interlocutions.
I also sensed at once that Canada
gave one space, not just geographical
but psychic, haunted by absence of ghosts,

a willing suspension of history
which suited me, with my rough overcoat
of inherited perplexities. So,
stay up all night if you need to, and I
did, arriving at morning seminars,
if not bright-eyed and bushy-tailed, at least
intimately prepared from reading all night.

Late one night, dissatisfied with my thesis,
knowing it would take a chunk of my soul,
and therefore better be well imagined,
conceived, adumbrated, I came across
a foreword in an edition of Clare,
mentioning that there was no book on him
as yet; I instantly knew my task was,
God willing, to write that book. From then on
each moment ticked away as ballast
towards that distant goal, how distant I
fortunately didn't reckon: I knew the why
but not the how, the when, or who's to pay.

Those half-remembered fallings-off to sleep
as Clare numbered the streaks of local tulips—
Dr. Johnson had famously argued
that the poet doesn't bother with streaks—
and crept through bramble bushes in pursuit
of nightingales, his patience rewarded
by finding empty nests among the grass,
impelled me forward to spend five years
studying his offbeat meanderings
in seemingly unromantic landscapes
of the Fen country, lowered horizons
giving him an insect's view of the world,
which he preferred to lucrative prospects,
in both senses of the word, refusing
his chief editor's advice to "raise his views,"
knowing that it was against his status

as a peasant poet without prospects.
"Shine, poet, in thy place, and be content"
wrote Wordsworth, not condescendingly,
meaning poetry ennobles every
station of life with authenticity.

Early in this quest, I borrowed an old bike
from a friend at Cambridge, and explored
the Dutch-like wide horizons of Rutland,
Northamptonshire with its slim pointed spires
at every middle distance, Cambridgeshire
with the massive profile of Ely
Cathedral beckoning one onwards
to spiritual and literary
salvation, pauses for country tea-shops,
wild bird-song everywhere, plus evensong
at occasional Anglican churches.
An art gallery of cloudscapes lit up
or darkened many an expedition—
Cuyp, Constable, Ruisdael, Crome, de Wint,
the latter a favourite of Clare's
from his nine-day-wonder days in London,
his discovery of painting, landscape
awareness, and the hidden ironies
of prospects, retrospects, and distances
lending enchantment to the tourist view;
for him, an insect grass-level vista
which only a madman would paint in depth,
a confrontation with the teeming life
of raw evolutionary nature.

Clare for a short time was an assistant
gardener at Burghley House, near Stamford,
one of the most beguiling towns in England.
I pedaled around the Capability
Brown landscape to get a feel for designed
nature, as opposed to virgin nature,

if there is such a thing in Fen country,
what with drainage schemes and enclosures.

The outdoor staff at Burghley were busy
preparing for the famous Horse Trials,
jumps being built, marquees in full rigging,
awaiting a rather more presentable
crowd than I must have seemed to lookers-on,
with bicycle clips and disheveled hair.

A week later I was back in Toronto,
where I was soon to meet a charming girl,
who was intrigued to meet an Irishman
who seemed to know about equestrian
events—as part of a former job,
he took students to Badminton as well—
she being, then as now, horse obsessed.
Perhaps it was this chat that made us click,
as two years later we were married,
and on our way to Oxford to explore
belovèd Clare more deeply. One never
knows the chance remarks that spin other folk
into our orbit, or have the reverse effect
of whirling our star off its steady course.

Sometimes idle chat becomes momentous,
stars aligned at an otherwise routine
party among assorted graduates
in one of the city's more nondescript
streets, Spadina Avenue. I also
remember that I was wearing a *crois*,
a knitted Celtic belt that was a gift
from Eoin O'Mahony, prodigal talker
and famous genealogist, who once
explained to me much about my own
family I had not known. A double-decker
bus lurching its way to Rathgar brought me

to a chance meeting with "The Pope", as he
was affectionately nicknamed—no one
knows why—on the upper deck I admired
his belt; he forthwith presented it
to me, hereafter to wear proudly,
not least on this auspicious occasion,
making belts and beasts our main talking points.

VI

The Cottage, Caulcott Lodge, Caulcott, Oxfordshire

While a graduate student at Pembroke,
I walk to the nearby Campion Hall
to meet Peter Levi, lover of Clare's
work. Tiny lodgings: I ask where he sleeps,
so he points to what looks like a dog's bed
in the corner, and laughs. An inspiring
companion, bright even by Oxford standards,
witty, charitable, compassionate;
he took me once to Mob Quad in Merton
College, the oldest quad in Oxford, where we
met Tom Stoppard, who was rehearsing one
of his plays for television, Peter
acting as interpreter for abstruse
classical references in the text.
Peter's moral sense was deep and humbling,
his presence a stimulus to decent
self-government and precision in language,
by the nineteen seventies a fading
breed, since so many of the newcomers
had no respect for history, language
in the rigorous traditional sense,
each word written or uttered subjected
to a rapid arrow-list of choices
to maximize precision, meaning, force,
eloquence an ingredient, not frill.

The new bureaucratic speech was arid,
loosely constructed, populist in its
immediate appeal, dying on the lips.
We talked of mayhem in Northern Ireland,
then at one of its most violent phases,
and I blurted out, "The situation
there is irredeemable." Peter cut
that short abruptly, "Nothing is beyond
redemption." I was morally ashamed
of my loose language, and promised myself
then and there never to let the anchor

of sane and reasonable speech to slip
into vagueness, ineptitude, conceit,
half-knowledge masquerading as the whole,
laziness to justify rash judgement.
Such moments should be part of the poet's
maturation, a dawning sense that words
are weapons, blunt, sharp, and murderous,
unless dissolved in the just crucible
of inner equilibrium, sharpened
in meaning but blunted with compassion,
that we make or damage our life with words
and have to swallow dictionaries whole.

Peter was widely and honourably
published, Penguin-selected poet, scholar
of Greek dialects and theology.
He epitomized for me that old lure
of Oxford, sometimes a drab, soul-heavy
place, sometimes living up to every dream
of Matthew Arnold's "tempestuous morn
in early June," with drifting blossom, scents
of full wisteria, cumulus clouds
edging along the rooftops, pinnacles,
golden stone suddenly made warm and soft
as choirs rehearse, and *les jeunes filles en fleurs*
balance books and ambitions on wobbly
bicycles, their gaunt beaux elegantly
kitted out for end-of-exam high jinks
before the slow encroachment of careers.

My wife and I made the most of our two
impecunious years, she doing light
cooking for the gentry, I driving in
the fourteen miles to read in libraries,
or see my tutor at Pembroke, editor
of Samuel Johnson, bow-tied, genial.
Thanks to Jennifer's frugal housekeeping,

steering me on the straight and narrow path,
avoiding the manifold temptations
of such a heady atmosphere of youth
and potentiality, keeping head
bent over the open page of many
books, scanned, skimmed or inwardly digested,
hoping to build a lasting balustrade
of the mind to overlook extensive
vistas of knowledge, as if in an Old
Master painting where distanced time and space
entice the viewer to grow would-be wings
to float over the goings-on below.

It was a time of wonderful friendships:
ah! to telephone Jon Stallworthy
at Oxford University Press, hear
that chipper voice, kind, intelligent,
it put one's whole week in sharp perspective.
Met first in Sligo, Jon could dissect lines
of poetry as skilfully as his
New Zealand surgeon father could bodies.
We were working through a passion for Yeats,
Jon signed a book: "For Tim, brother-in-Yeats."

Francis Warner, with his huge ambition
to build a Beckett theatre at Saint Peter's
College, under the quadrangle. Francis
had what his master at Christ's Hospital,
Edward Malins, called a huge *os frontis*,
a sparkling, if erratic, intelligence.
Another Yeatsian, first met at Sligo,
Francis was a dynamo of learning.

Malins himself, *"un homme qu'on ne fait
plus à Londres"*, wrote brilliant books
on literature and landscape, how both were
inter-related in certain eras,
rich compost for my gestating Clare book.

Many highlights float up like swaying buoys
on the shifting tides of memory:
the memorial service for Auden
at Christ Church, Stephen Spender orating,
"The Ode to Saint Cecilia" set by
Benjamin Britten, magically sung,
two masterpieces for the price of one,
provoking a sharp catch in the throat;
an organ recital in Merton Chapel
by Stephen Cleobury, later
in charge of music at King's, Cambridge,
the mediaeval acoustics at Merton
equal to King's with its soaring fan vaults.
A May ball at Merton, a slow, pale dawn
etching Magdalen Tower on the cold sky.
That evening was a rare treat snatched from time:
I had just returned from Ireland, where I
had gone to collect some furniture
left me by my mother—the rented van
had proved impossible, not going more
than thirty miles per hour, its lights kaput,
so I had a hair-raising drive from Wales
as dusk fell over the shifting landscape,
my right arm grossly swollen from a sting
inflicted by bees as I helped a friend's
father in Wicklow. Back safely, my wife
ran a hot bath, and I sank gratefully
into it, as she pulled up the car,
in which we were to drive to Oxford.
Setting off, the undercarriage snapped,
and we were stranded, so pushing it to
the side, we walked to the station, and got
the last train into Oxford, arriving
already exhausted, just before midnight,
and gulped our supper, and told our tall tales,
glad to be alive and in one piece.

The French have a phrase describing post-war
intellectual style: *les trente années
glorieuses*. To us, it was just normal,
but looking back, we were inhabitants,
unseeing, of a rare mind-gilded age:
MacDowell at Trinity College, Dublin,
a true eccentric, natural talker,
whose influence reached beyond his discipline,
history, into the farthest niches
of society, his witticisms,
his endless ability to create
laughter, intentional or not, retailed
in countless grateful reminiscences.

An Oxford legend, Sir Isaiah
Berlin was the living embodiment
of European culture: his rapid-
fire lectures, all conflicting values,
the epitome of a first-class mind.
At a conference on Romanticism,
one question came: "What about the Noble
Savage?" Berlin's answer rattled on for
twenty minutes; I wished myself Boswell,
as no one now could understand the speed
and range of speakers of that period.

Sir Kenneth Clark of *Civilisation*
fame came to the Oxford Union to talk
about famous people he had known; I
asked him afterwards what he thought of Jack
Yeats, knowing that Clark had met his famous
poet brother: he drily said, "He couldn't
draw," consigning him at a single stroke
to an also-ran in the pantheon
that includes Ingres and Leonardo;
W.B. is still in the top rank.

Lord Longford, known then as Lord Porn,
since he was Chair of an inquest into
pornography, was a restrained, cogent
speaker, another first-class mind, Labour
peer in the days when Harold Wilson's team
included six first-class Oxford degrees,
and at a time when such an achievement
was universally recognizable,
its hallmarks clarity, eloquence, huge
reach of allusion, and reference across
cultures and languages and centuries.

When I was preparing my John Clare book
for the Clarendon Press on Walton Street—
greeted by a porter in livery—
I spent two intensely focused hours
with my copy editor at the press,
a formidably erudite woman,
who noticed if a comma had slipped its
moorings, or pounced on words used a tad too
cavalierly; that session with her brought
to mind our sergeant-major gym teachers
at my first boarding school, fresh from the war,
so determined to beat good physical
moves into us, no room for self-esteem.
In the long run, such people did us proud,
as they caught ineptitudes, so one could
face the critics and the begrudgers
with a clear text and a firm context.

VII

Fairbridge Drive, Duncan, British Columbia

Long a lover of old Chinese paintings,
tiny figures in a jagged landscape
of mountains, with wispy mists or clouds
suspended half-way up the long canvas,
I was overjoyed to see Pacific
landscapes in the flesh, as my wife and I
trekked west for ten days, five thousand miles,
the steaks getting thicker in each province,
and sure enough, there were those half-way clouds.
Yesterday, the Canada geese flew past
squawking, skimming the tops of our cedars,
unlike the east-coast geese, who fly high up
in the Atlantic storm-ridden sky-scape.

But then life took another of its twists,
and tried to root out the spiritual
fibres I had thought inviolable.
Led by French intellectual logic-
choppers, literati began to sneer
at one's love of beauty in the spoken
and written word, denied the eminence
of poetry, ignored the building-up
of verbal interest in the deep mind,
a process analogous to money
accumulating in a bank account—
perhaps it was a reaction to this
seemingly capitalist metaphor—
in any case, for several decades
ideology and jargon stifled
the fresh winds of inspirational words,
the heritage of English-language work
pre-eminent among the nations,
not least because of the Irish writers.
English is a rich hotchpotch of many
roots: Greek, Latin, Saxon, Danish, Norman
French, its etymology created
by invasion and assimilation,

poets, scholars, and many dialects.
What was a writer to do, when critics
told us that traditional writing styles
deserved to be sent to Siberia,
or at least Coventry, that collective
issues were to be foregrounded, Dickens
and the glorious idiosyncrasies
of his characters dispersed in blandness?

Modern society has become, some say,
more and more mechanical: the left brain
has tilted the scales relentlessly down
in its favour, leaving the things poets
value out in the cold. What is this loss?
Dissociation of sensibility
indeed, hard to describe in an essay
when one was young, but borne out day by day
of one's experience, so much more than
the perennial blunting of youthful
exuberance, common throughout the ages,
but a denaturing, a reduction
of sensuous pleasure, the very soil
of one's emotions deprived of nurture,
just as soil itself is impoverished.
The left brain has an over-exalted
opinion of itself, hard to deny.
Why is it hard to defend the best things?
Has language been stripped of profundity
so radically that the poet's job
has become an archaeologist's dig
to find long-buried shards of amplitude,
the full-bellied sail of past impulses?

Farewell all subtlety, implicitness,
connotation, metaphorical truth,
suspect to the utilitarian,
the narrow-gauge railroaded attitude

of mainstream-educated know-it-alls.
Long live that old dream-gifted balance
of flow and stasis, of intuition
and tuition, of true whole-heartedness,
quality and equality as one,
so rare to achieve except in great art,
that reverberation sought by baroque
harpsichordists, the flow and poise of dance
that drives even Bach's most mortality-
obsessed arias and cantatas,
all hard contradictions sublimated:
contexts providing texts with texture.

For words can obscure truth as well as light
the way, words can bludgeon and stultify
our sensibilities, can sensitize
or desensitize our responses, root
up our traditions or settle them in;
they used to be at the epicentre
of education, of enlightenment,
but we lost our faith in deep eloquence,
lost the courage to tell it like it is,
or at least intuit the truth as we
see it. But truth is never popular,
and it certainly never made money,
so gradually meaning eroded,
our minds, hearts, guts all parted company,
as if they could do without each other.
We lost respect for language, and our fear
of its nefarious effects blunted.
Poets became an endangered species,
although much poetry remained in print,
but the public back-up and double thumbs-up
became a grudging nervous amusement
at their antics, a Dylan Thomas or
a Brendan Behan at least could fuel
scurrilous copy if not sell their works.

Then in the popular mind élitism
became a no-no, which spelled certain death
to much good work, as who wants to be seen
as an enemy of the people?
A friend of mine keeps asking, who is your
audience? Impossible to answer,
as one writes as if every awake mind
would understand what one is getting at.
But between the writing and the reading
falls the shadow, as T.S. Eliot
so memorably implied, a giant mind
such as his should know, and lesser poets
also learn. Poetry is perennial,
it will keep returning on its silver
wheels like Tennyson's dawn, even if few
ears can hear it. Poetry must reject
too much mouthing of easy sentiment
as if life were all one journalistic
cliché and down-dumbing *ressentiment.*

In one of my favourite Latin tags:
"We bees make honey, but not for ourselves,"—
what a muscled word *mellificamus*:
Latin is poetry, you have to dig
meaning out of compression, from the soil
of layer upon layer of strata.
There I go, two long foreign expressions
within four lines: am I not being snobbish
and élitist? Well, I'll take the rap, it's
up to the reader to decide, readers
come in every possible embodiment;
one cannot write as if one were a chef
catering to every culinary
whim, and if you do not like my diction,
at least I won't literally poison you.

"The lyf so short, the craft so long to lerne";
one always knew that by a wise instinct,

but in later life one is always shocked
at how true it is: now Eavan Boland
has joined the shades, her reputation made.
I first met her when she was nineteen,
a feisty young red-head, who seemed to know
her own mind at the very starting-post,
eager to take on the male-heavy
tradition, which still treated its women
as objective icons like the Virgin Mary,
figureheads, not creative pioneers.
We walked the streets, chanting myriad lines
of Yeats, that unavoidable giant
whose ghost had to be tussled with before
one could find one's own independent voice.
It was still the early sixties, that air
of change for good, of new diversity,
especially in time-worn provincial
Ireland, always a pale mirror of what
was happening elsewhere—a friend of Yeats
described Dublin as a "shabby England"—
but shabbiness was being fast eclipsed by
a future-grabbing get-up-and-go-ness,
a euphoric period when Ireland seemed
to be escaping its tragic destiny,
drilled into us by history, instinct,
and foreboding, when Dublin seemed to be
returning to the vivid faces
of Yeats's poems, but without the violence.
It didn't last long, animosities
in the North revealed an unhealed soul-wound
that demanded human sacrifice.
Literary relevance moved North,
Heaney, Mahon, Longley in the vanguard
but all with a foothold in the South.

So what should the French do with Notre Dame?
Make it a temple of Reason, à la

Rousseau, or topple the whole damn thing
to make a car park? Very few would like
the latter option, but conservation
is time-consuming and expensive, needs
communal support and many experts:
many journalists thought the monarchy
had copped it when we saw the billows rise
from the towers of Windsor Castle,
but the nation rallied, and solutions
were found, and brilliantly carried forward.
But what we learned was not just that Brits
love their country, but that such monuments
are embodied in the general sub-
consciousness, that in a mysterious
way we would all be the poorer losing
the flying buttresses and ritual
of these artefacts created by time.
You don't need to be a monarchist, Christian,
or anything else to feel that buildings
and all they configure are essential
representations of humanity,
that if the Taj Mahal were to be lost,
humanity would be impoverished.

Which brings one to the question of Beauty:
no one can once and for all define
it, but it would be a sad day to hear
that beauty had been banned, that no one
was to strive for its distant blandishments,
that it was an unforgivable pride
in hierarchy, distinction, and expense
of spiritual capital to hoist
such hubristic edifices again.
Like most arguments, this one is pointless
in all important aspects of life:
we don't form committees to fall in love,
or if we did, love itself would falter.

For consumerism obliterates
wonder and humility, ingredients
our ancestors had in plenty, lacking
our comfortable and pampered settings.
Does one inevitably drive the other
out? Does affluence extinguish spirit?
Imponderable questions without clear
answers, but the door to knowledge is prised
open by questioning, so that there are sure
to be further rooms in the mind's mansion
for Keatsian maiden chambers and more,
always new neural connections to be
made and spiral staircases to be scaled,
look-out parapets to be constructed,
and attics to be forever rummaged.

"Who is this that darkeneth counsel
by words without knowledge?" Thus the *Book of Job*.
Use words that take the light, not darken it;
easy to say, hard enough to practice,
but every poet should have it as goal,
when the darkness of mass opinion rules.
Beckett was scarified by many things,
but the human mind reduced to bedrock,
mechanical, slick, humourless, witless—
Coleridge's Imagination dead—
was probably his worst antagonist.
He kept his appointment with words, so sparse,
so elemental, they could not but be strong.

Poets, take Izaak Walton's phrase to heart:
"Study to be quiet," as quoted in
the stained-glass window in Winchester
Cathedral. Carry the impoverished
spirit of language back to its fibrous
origins, let its far-asunder roots
explore rich soil again, exfoliate,
to be a quick candelabra of bloom.

Epiphany. Useful word from James Joyce
and Holy Writ. Wherever. For me it
means those rarest moments when everything
comes together, when years of slog and slog
slough off, leaving a pure distillation
of sensation, feeling, emotion fused
into meaningfulness; just this morning
on my way down the gravel pathway steps
to gather in some clean laundry, crisp-dried
in the early autumn sun, I looked back
and far from being turned to pillar-salt
I saw our ripening Melrose apples,
baroque clouds forming and reforming over
the slanted rooftops, roses, geraniums,
full-blown hydrangeas, the pretty lace-caps
nodding in a slight breeze, and gratitude
welled up unbidden from its hidden lair.

*Acknowledgements
&
A Note about the Author*

Acknowledgements

My sister, Rosemary MacGillycuddy, has been an invaluable source of the intricacies of family history; her memory is sharp and tenacious.

Jonathan Williams has been an astute, generous and genial advisor for many years.

Ron Smith, former owner/publisher at Oolichan Books, has been a wise and knowledgeable reader, and an unrivalled guide.

Gloria Lorenzen has provided many fruitful conversations, and has given detailed feedback on many occasions.

Joan Mortin has been supportive of the project throughout, and has been "hearer and heartener of the work."

Thanks to Gary Geddes, who gave a detailed assessment of the work at an early stage.

Thanks to Antony Farrell of the Lilliput Press for his interest.

My thanks to the following friends, who have seen the work at various stages and whose comments have sharpened my involvement with the text: Marcus Beresford; Christopher Bielenberg; John Bielenberg; Rivers Carew; David and Delia Denyer; Patrick Kelly; Conor MacGillycuddy; Connie Milbrath; Oscar Pelta; Bill Somerville-Large.

My greatest debt, as always, is to my wife Jennifer; she is the greatest blessing of my adult life.

A Note about the Author

Timothy Brownlow is Emeritus Professor of English Literature at Vancouver Island University. Born in Dublin, he graduated in Modern Languages (English and French) from Trinity College, Dublin in 1963; he also received a Higher Diploma in Education in 1965 and an M.A. in 1969 from Trinity. He edited *Icarus*, the literary magazine ("a well-sustained and well-expressed editorial policy" (*Irish Times*), and he co-edited *The Dublin Magazine* for six years with Rivers Carew. This was described in *The Times* (London) as "Ireland's leading literary quarterly" and the reviewer for *The Irish Times* wrote: "A really alive, serious, contemporary magazine." The reviewer in *Hibernia* wrote that "it has become known as a magazine of high quality ... the editors are performing a notable service to Irish letters by editing this magazine." From 1963 to 1969, Brownlow taught at his former school, Saint Columba's College, County Dublin.

Brownlow completed a doctorate in English in 1975 at York University, Toronto, having spent two years of his research as a Migrant Graduate at Pembroke College, Oxford. He received the Queen Elizabeth Ontario Scholarship in 1972, and he was a Killam Post-Doctoral Fellow at Dalhousie University from 1975 to 1978. A revised version of his thesis on John Clare was later published by the Clarendon Press, Oxford, as *John Clare and Picturesque Landscape* (1983); Nina Auerbach in *Studies in English Literature* wrote: "Clare is studied with rich and acute understanding in Timothy Brownlow's wonderful [book]. This is the best study of Clare yet written; ... it fuses personal with political understanding."

His collection of sonnets and other poems, *Climbing Croagh Patrick*, was published by Oolichan Books, British Columbia, in 1998. W. J. Keith was "deeply impressed by the civilised sincerity of these poems" (*Canadian Book Review Annual*, 2000). Oolichan Books also published a collection of essays, *Hiding Places*, in 2008, described by Eric Miller in *The Malahat Review* as revealing "a conscience magnanimous, troubled, vulnerable to beauty, pluralistic, and eloquent."

Brownlow's work, both poetry and scholarship, is represented in the following anthologies: *The Penguin Book of Irish Verse* (1970, 1982); *Poems for Clare* (Clare Society, UK, 1998); an article, "A Molehill for Parnassus: John Clare and Prospect Poetry," published in *University of Toronto Quarterly* (1979) and reprinted in *The Critical Perspective*, edited by Harold Bloom (Chelsea House, New York)—this article was also republished in an anthology published by Gage; *In Fine Form: the Canadian Book of Form Poetry* (Raincoast Books, British Columbia, 2005); an essay about Irish food appeared in *Apples Under the Bed* (Hedgerow Press, 2007). His work is featured in the June 2007 issue of *Poetry Ireland Review*.

In his retirement, Tim has taught numerous courses for Lifelong Learners in Duncan, British Columbia; has taught three courses and given a public lecture at the downtown Vancouver campus of Simon Fraser University; and he has acted as President of the Vancouver Island Branch of the Alumni Association of Trinity College, Dublin (2009–2015).

"Only Connect," an article on teaching Romanticism, appears in an online anthology, "Romanticism, Ecology, and Pedagogy," published by the Romantic Circles Pedagogy Commons [www.rc.umd.edu/pedagogies/commons/ecology/].

www.ingramcontent.com/pod-product-compliance
Lightning Source LLC
Chambersburg PA
CBHW060401080526
44583CB00012B/427